Awakening the Performing Body

Consciousness Literature the & Arts 17

Awakening the Performing Body

JADE ROSINA McCUTCHEON

Amsterdam - New York, NY 2008

Cover Design:
Aart Jan Bergshoeff

Cover illustration: photograph by Corrie Ancone

The paper on which this book is printed meets the requirements of "ISO 9706:1994, Information and documentation - Paper for documents - Requirements for permanence".

ISBN: 978-90-420-2431-1
ISSN: 1573-2193
©Editions Rodopi B.V., Amsterdam - New York, NY 2008
Printed in the Netherlands

For Joana and Barbara

Table of Contents

Acknowledgements

I would like to thank and acknowledge the many people who have contributed to this book over the past eleven years. Firstly the people at the heart of the work are the many actors and students who graciously engaged their adventurous spirit. They are: Theatre Media students at Charles Sturt University, Bathurst; professional actors from Sydney for the *Alabama Rain* project; MFA and undergraduate actors from University of California, Davis; actors from the Actors Centre, Sydney and participants in the workshops at many IFTR (International Federation of Theatre Research) conferences. To Daniel Meyer- Dinkgräfe, Barbara Sellers-Young, Jennifer Fisher, Ben Bradley, Jane Selby, Dean Carey, Mary Elizabeth Anderson I give my heartfelt thanks for your unending faith, support and belief in the work. I would like to thank Jean-Pierre Voos who opened my eyes to the power of theatre and to all the KISS members with whom I shared my earliest deep dives into the nature of being, you are all part of this work.

I am very grateful to the Office of the Vice Chancellor for Research and the Division of Humanities, Arts and Cultural Studies, University of California, Davis for the Publication Assistance grant.

I would like to acknowledge Suzanne Ingleton and Kerry Dwyer as two Australian actor/directors who really pioneered much of the thinking behind the acting approach in this book. Thank you for your generosity and wonderful teaching, both to me and the actors you taught.

This book would not exist without the continued support of the two university departments I have taught in (School of Communication, Charles Sturt University, Bathurst, New South Wales and The Department of Theatre and Dance, University of California. Davis) and the people I have worked closely with in the development of these exercises. I would like to thank Martha Rehrman for her support, attention to detail and proof reading of the book.

Without the loving support and guidance of my mother Joana McCutcheon, Mary-Faeth Chenery and Gale Orford who mentored me in the early stages of this work, I would never have discovered the Theosophical connections to Stanislavsky's work and another language for the interpretation of spirit.

I thank Andrew White for his scholarship and collegial sharing and support and John Galland for his inspiration and encouragement. Finally I particularly thank Daniel Meyer-Dinkgräfe for his continuous mentoring, support and guidance over the last decade.

Preface

Patrice Pavis suggests in his book, *Theatre at the Crossroads of Culture* that cultural sources are widespread, thousands of years old, often passed on by word of mouth and then recorded by many different voices. Theatre has been influenced by this process as previous styles of performance have been adapted for new historical contexts. Artaud was deeply influenced by Balinese performance, Ann Bogart by the physical regimes of Tadashi Suzuki, Brecht by the performance of Mei Lan Fang and the list goes on. In Australia, particularly in the 80's, the work of many new theatre makers as well as that of the established 'alternative' and 'avant garde' contributed to an exploration of form. Companies such as *Legs on the Wall, The Sydney Front* (now disbanded), *Zen Zen Zo, Australian Fruit Fly* and many others established a more physical style of story telling. When the Chinese Circus trained the Australian Fruit Fly Circus in Albury in the early 1980's, they revised the training of the Australian circus performers with the addition of an increased sense of focus and discipline. Along with the sharing of different cultural approaches to performer and actor training comes an accompanying difference of consciousness which invariably affects the existing cultural consciousness in the performer.

This book continues this interweaving of various constructions of consciousness associated with conceptions of the spiritual, mystical and shamanic. Moving ideas across terrain that is occupied by constructions of thought spanning centuries is tricky, especially when it involves citing different cultures as key inspirations. Using a word such as 'shamanic' invokes problematic layers of interpretation; using the word 'spiritual' again brings with it a set of difficulties, 'soul' and 'sacred' also bring us to other sites of discourse that immediately colour the place of actor training.

Language is a double-edged sword, accessing us to wonderful places and creating obstacles and barriers at the same time, I hope the design of words in the following chapters might allow for some space between the landscapes attached to words like; 'shamanic, spiritual, soul and sacred', providing perhaps the possibility of new words to come which may bring us closer to creating a dialogue about energy exchange in the theatre between bodies and the altered states that emerge from this unique transaction.

The exercises in this book have been developed as a result of explorations in rehearsal and acting classes. In an attempt to discover words that might assist us as actor trainers, actors and performers to open up some paths into the metaphysic layer of performance I have drawn on words and language from other cultures that come closest to defining the quality of the exercise and or philosophy behind the exercise. They are informed by experience and ideas from various texts on Theosophy, Shamanism and the Chakras rather than coming directly from any native or shamanic traditions, customs or beliefs. The Body Energy Centre work is informed by the Chakra system but not developed from any specific system. It is important to keep in mind that these exercises and approaches are developed for actors and are not intended to be systems of learning or belief systems that would operate outside the rehearsal and actor training spaces.

A note on the representation of gender in this book.

I have struggled with how to best represent both genders in a balanced way throughout this book without creating a distraction from the text for the reader. I believe if one is referred to as 'her' or 'she' throughout her life she should see this reflected in all literature at least 50% of the time, instead of having to translate 'he' and 'his' constantly as possibly meaning 'her'. As a solution (admittedly not the ideal one), I have referred to the actor as male in the Introduction and Chapters Two and Four and female in Chapters One, Three and Five. Where authors are quoted who have used the old form of 'his', I will not add 'sic' after each occasion.

Introduction

What creates the audience/performer dynamic? How does an actor negotiate the site of energy exchange between breathing bodies in various stages of consciousness? This dynamic lies at the core of the act of theatre. Originally this work investigated the training of actors in our culture and whether this training enhanced the audience/performer dynamic. Eleven years later the rescarch has evolved into a potential actor training methodology called at this stage Body Energy Work. The journey over the past eleven years with like minded practitioners, students and professional actors in Australia and undergraduate and graduate actors in the United States has been informed, tantalized and shaped by many different theoretical, academic, philosophical and practical approaches to the extraordinary art of acting.

As I investigated what this energetic space was between the audience and the actor I realized that part of the answer to the above questions lay in the way we train actors – (I just accepted at the time that training the audience was out of the question although today I am not so sure about that). The question then became how can you train actors in way that enhances the actor/audience connection? The rest of the journey has remained entirely focused on this enquiry and at the time of writing this book is still very much 'in process'.

Working with many actors from different schools of training I explored exercises drawn from disciplines and schools of thought that dealt largely with ideas and philosophies spun around 'energy' and 'forces' that we can feel and know but not see. I was amazed to discover as I researched that practitioners like Stanislavsky and Chekhov were very influenced by the esoteric sciences, unseen energies, metaphysics, yoga, meditation and theosophy.

When Constantin Stanislavsky searched for a way to bring what he considered 'truth' to the stage he was responding to the truth of the presence of a person in the early 1900s. His perspective of truth was gauged by his levels of consciousness and perception, which were colored by the time in which he lived. It is true that much of his work still relates and resonates today as he was exploring a more essential aspect of a person. However, our awareness and understanding of the possibilities of who we are have evolved and developed in the last one hundred years. Through the discoveries and investigations of psychology, science, archeology, sociology and consciousness studies we have a vast terrain of possibilities of 'self.'

As the work developed, actors provided feedback on these ways of working, often confirming that these aspects had always been present with them but they had not had the language with which to express this in the rehearsal room. Indeed, most directors I spoke with responded in a similar way, that there was no language in the current actor training programs that can be used to facilitate the development within the actor of an 'audience response-ability' via the energy body.

First, the actor needed to develop this vocabulary and develop their inner body energies before they could begin to work with the audience's energies. The work in this book is at this stage, training actors to develop a palate of terms and experiences with which they can develop another layer of Body Energy Work. One of the results of this work is a journey for the actor into the deeper parts of self in which they could discover a 'purer state of being' or a state that encompassed the energetic layers of self as well as the physical, mental and emotional.

Possibly this search for a 'purer state of being' is not so unlike Stanislavsky's search for truth in his time. When he saw that the representation of a person on stage was a far cry from what he perceived to be the 'real' state of a person in life, then he was driven to create a system of training that would assist the actor in a closer representation or a more truthful representation of a person on stage. Perhaps with the changing nature of what a person is, actor training is constantly trying to adapt its structures of training, which in turn affect the way a person is represented. As we are surrounded by images of 'self' portrayed by actors who are trained by these methods, it seems a logical progression for actor training techniques and approaches to keep up with the evolving nature of people and their connected levels of consciousness and perception.

Many actors cannot articulate the process of their intuition, instinct or imagination, yet they can describe the process of identifying the motivation and action for the character via script analysis. Some actors, it seems, can read the energy of the audience and play to that energy. How does this occur? Does the actor read thought forms, energy states or auras? We know from scientific and anthropological research that communication via thought forms exists; often described as 'telepathy'. What if the actor were trained in telepathy- is this possible?

Proving telepathy exists is like trying to see the wind or photographing electricity as it flies through the lines above and below us; we have entire religious systems and beliefs based on energy we cannot see or validate scientifically. The actor's intuition cannot be captured scientifically either, yet every actor I know draws on unseen energies within and around their body to practice their craft.

Part of the difficulty is to identify this unseen energy with language that does not bind it to religion or 'new ageist' cults. This unseen energy is an aware energy with a consciousness borne of the sources it emanates from, as opposed to electricity, which does not carry awareness in terms of consciousness. How do we language this non-physical, aware live energy so an actor can begin to develop a mastery of this consciousness?

The approach to acting in this book explores and works with the many levels of consciousness experienced by the actor, both in rehearsal and performance. It offers exercises to train the actor to develop the possibility of consciously manipulating the audi-ence/performer dynamic by working with thought forms, unseen energies and radiations from the body. What happens between the body of the audience and the body of the performer? Do we experience a certain level of shared consciousness, move into altered

1   2

states beyond ourselves, project and transfer our notion of 'self' onto the performing body?

I walk onstage and instead of an empty space, bare floorboards and theatre walls, I see an orchard; it is spring with a warm breeze and the sound of a bird singing. I am 32 but really 45. I am in the year 1894 but really 2005. I am engaged for the first time but really married with two children. All of this 'performing self' is an illusion, an imagined state, a series of thought forms so strong and so focused they reach across a boundary and draw in the other who willingly contributes to the thought form, an act of suspended disbelief.

If anything, theatre is an act of communal dreaming, a site of collective consciousness where invisible energies of life forces intermingle, interact and connect. The connecting medium between bodies, whatever we may call it, can be affected by our thoughts, state of awareness and consciousness. In some ways the actors and audience become part of one dynamic network in which many feelings, thoughts and awareness's are shared.

The idea of 'becoming one' with everything in our space rather than being separate is a concept Jung explored through the state of *unus mundus,* described as a "psychological event by which man becomes one with everything existing"[1]. According to Jung, when one achieves the state of *unus mundus*, one is part of all that exists. The outer is one with the inner and ego and consciousness become part of the collective unconscious.

The rise of Theosophy through Madam Helene Blavatsky (1831-1891) generated many books interpreting and re-interpreting the ideas of 'subtle bodies' and 'planes of existence'. One might view these concepts as layers of consciousness in present terms. In 1927 A.E. Powell wrote "Briefly, the astral body (of man) is a vehicle not unlike the physical body...composed of matter finer than that of physical matter, in which feelings, passions, desires and emotions are

---

[1] Von Franz 1979: 17.

expressed and which acts as a bridge or medium between the physical body and the higher mind."[2]

Arthur Powell's book on the Astral Body may assist us in understanding (or languaging) the ability of an actor to 'reach into' and affect the world of the audience, to touch an audience member with this projected energy. Powell describes this ability as the radiation of vibrations connected to higher thought forms.[3]

He describes how 'radiating thought forms' create seas of thoughts through which we wander daily, and that visions and apparitions are actually manifestations of very strong thought forms. The application of this information is the potential ability for the actor to consciously send thought forms into the audience via the astral body. When Powell states, "In fact, there are on the astral plane vast numbers of thought forms of a comparatively permanent character, often the result of the cumulative work of generations of people,"[4] he could well be referring to an aspect of Jung's notion of the collective unconscious. Accordingly, the more an actor dwells in the thought forms of his character, the stronger these forms become.

Chekhov's technique of radiation is an exercise of 'projecting energy' from body to body. This exercise develops awareness in the actor of unseen present energies that he can use as part of his extended body. The actor's consciousness, the knowing self, is an expanded awareness of energy beyond the physical. These energies can form an almost palpable etheric web, linking the actors and audience together in the same physical space. This act becomes a sharing of the altered space, not unlike the sharing of energies in a church, a ceremony, a ritual or a 'rave' dance. *Communal energy as ritual.*

To be conscious of these energies means developing what I call 'shamanic consciousness', to work with the unseen forces around you with clear intent.

---

[2] Powell 1982: 1.
[3] Ibid. 44.
[4] Ibid. 54.

Language is also an important part of the journey to the inner self for an actor; it establishes boundaries and permissions, walking tracks and markers that enable the actor to recognize and remember the journey, bringing back new and rich information about the character or himself.

Philip Auslander writes, "Theorists as diverse as Stanislavsky, Brecht and Grotowski all implicitly designate the actor's self as the *logos* of performance; all assume that the actor's self precedes and grounds his performance and that it is the presence of this self in performance that provides the audience with access to human truths"[5]. Thus the concept of 'self' for the actor needs to be interrogated on behalf of the audience. The 'self' today is a landscape of potential dimensions ranging from a shamanic idea of an eternal energetic self to a local physical body self.

With each acting exercise, consciousness is altered as the body, emotions, breathing and the way we see things also change. From one moment to the next, an actor becomes altered by the exercises he engages in, experiencing different states of awareness and consciousness. Each revolving state of consciousness might be seen as a horse on a carnival carousel revolving around and around the centre of self which is at the centre of the carousel. How then, does he prevent his 'body' from becoming a disoriented whirling globe of personas that appear random when he carries out these exercises? Logically, there must be a centre of self we return to after exploring these different states and characters.

What is the centre beyond these worlds of changeable selves? Surely, that is the place an actor most needs to find, a place from which to come regardless of the 'windows' of the body he is viewing the world through. We could think of these different aspects of self as layers around a core and that our consciousness and awareness are connected to that core. Once we are inside that core or centre we can then sit back and observe. The challenge of reaching this core self of both focused and extended consciousness is, I'm sure, familiar to most actors and actor trainers. Once we move beyond the outer layers

---

[5] Auslander 1995: 60.

of noise, what is it that we move to? Perhaps a central core of self from which we allow and observe the full spectrum of ourselves?

The removal of distractions, tensions, thoughts, nerves, the daily body and anything that is deemed to be in the way of the pure or neutral self has been a constant key factor in actor training approaches across the spectrum. Robert Forman stated in 1998, "Usually our minds are an enormously complex stew of thoughts, feelings, sensations, wants, snatches of song, pains, drives, daydreams and, of course, consciousness itself more or less aware of it all. To understand consciousness *in itself*, the obvious thing would be to clear away as much of this internal detritus and noise as possible"[6].

This technique is inspired by the body of actor training practitioners like Constantin Stanislavsky, Michael Chekhov, Jerzy Grotowski and Antonin Artaud who have acknowledged, through various terms, the importance of clearing away 'as much of this internal detritus and noise as possible'. It also considers various relaxation techniques derived from eastern systems such as Tai Chi, yoga and meditation, which we now know influenced each of these practitioners. If we are so influenced today by the work of these practitioners who engaged in a regular use of the words 'soul' and 'spirit', why wouldn't we be investigating what these words mean to the actor?

1. Stanislavsky: "In every role, at every show the actor must create not just the conscious but also the unconscious part of the life of the human spirit....only a tenth of our life is lived on a conscious plane".[7]

2. Chekhov: "When I try to imagine what the theatre can be and will be in the future (I speak neither in the mystical or religious sense at the moment), it will be a purely spiritual business in which the spirit of the human being will be

---

[6] Robert K.C. Forman 1998: 185-201.
[7] Stanislavsky 1962: 166, 167.

rediscovered by artists.....The actor must know what it is and how to take it and use it".[8]

3. Artaud: "Belief in the soul's flowing substantiality is essential to the actor's craft.....To know there is a physical outlet for the soul permits him to journey down into that soul".[9]

4. Grotowski: "The actor must not illustrate but accomplish an 'act of the soul' by means of his own organism".[10]

The words 'soul' and 'spirit', as suggested in the preface, are difficult to interpret. However, David Abram suggests that the word 'soul' has its roots in ancient Greek and Latin where the same word means 'soul', breath, 'wind' and 'air'. Abram also parallels with the Sanskrit word 'atman' used for 'soul', 'air' and 'breath', and suggests that throughout many cultures soul equals 'breath' or 'air' and this is what fills us with a life force and unites us all.[11]

I find this way of describing soul very useful as it relates strongly to the idea of breath, which is an area of focus within actor training and certainly a key element in the exercises within this book.

The technique is divided into three parts:

1.   Body Energy Centres (BECs). Chapters 2 & 3
2.   Shamanic Meditation Journeying. Chapter 4
3.   Playing the Exchange. Chapter 5

---

[8] Chekhov 1985: 140.

[9] Artaud 1997: 90.

[10] Grotowski's Statement of Principles, number three. 1968: 211-21.

[11] David Abram Ph.D. is an ecologist and philosopher. He wrote *The Spell of the Sensuous* in 1996 from which these references to soul were taken. Abram: 1996: 231, 238.

1. Body Energy Centre (BEC) Work

BEC work is a series of exercises with which to focus the energies of the body so characters can be created by using informed choices of combinations of Centres. The actor gets to know his body and how the energy Centres work through specific exercises. Once the actor understands which Centres are closed, leaking or open, he will then have the opportunity to explore these Centres and to create a more neutral body from which to draw the character. For example, if the actor Tom has a closed Belly Energy Centre (BEC) but has to play a character with a strong sexual or sensual nature, he will need to explore and understand the energy in this Centre before he can embody a desirable choice for the creation of a believable character. After working with this Centre for weeks, Tom will be able to open, close or leak energy from this Centre by choice.

An actor engaging in Heart and Mind Centres can produce a caring, visionary character; Belly BEC and Root BEC can help manifest a basic, violent and sexually motivated character. Using the Crown BEC alone can create an "off the planet" character. For example, in the play *Hedda Gabler* by Ibsen, the character of Hedda Gabler can be developed around mostly Mind and Solar Plexus energy Centres; however, when Lovberg appears, her Belly BEC and Heart BEC are activated which opens up the sexual and loving energies. When in the company of Brack, her Solar BEC is stronger and when with Tesman her Mind BEC takes over. Each line of text can be spoken through a different Energy Centre depending on the context. The ideal would be for actors to become user friendly with these Energy Centres in their body, dancing from one to the other in response to other characters, text and actions. The voice and posture are quite notably affected when an actor speaks from different Centres.

2. Shamanic Journeying

Considering the actor as a shaman comes in response to the need for re-clarification of consciousness with the aim of establishing a greater potential of representation of self. The idea of self then becomes one that is forever evolving and journeying into new states, although always connected to a Centre. The information gathered by anthropologists on shamanic rituals suggests that shamans typically journey into altered states with full awareness, which is why I use the words 'shamanic journeying' for this exercise.

It has been noted by anthropologists such as Victor Turner and Mircea Eliade, as well as theatre practitioners and theorists that an altered state can often occur during performance rituals in indigenous societies, often referred to as trance. In order to journey to the other dimensions of existence, a shaman induces an altered state of consciousness in himself, which is similar to a state of self-hypnosis. While in this shamanic trance he is in complete control, able to take consciousness into non-physical reality, where he visits the alternative realms of existence, communicates with and controls spirits, gains information, retrieves souls, and makes subtle changes in reality that may affect the physical world.[12]

The actor often experiences a trance-like consciousness on stage and in rehearsal, where a part of himself, what Chekhov called the 'Higher I', watches another part playing the character. "As one part of Chekhov's consciousness watched and gave commands to the character, another part of his consciousness performed as the character."[13] The actor is in control in an altered state; a 'self' able to identify and manipulate 'unseen' energies, or at least those 'unseen' by the observers or audience, he is acting on behalf of today's 'tribe' as a sportsman of the etheric.

Like the traditional shaman, the actor learns to master the energy fields like an etheric acrobat dancing with the forces between the bodies of all present in the act of theatre. While in an altered state or light shamanic trance, he is in complete control, able to take consciousness into non-physical reality where he visits the alternative realms of existence. He is a magician of unseen forces, creating rich and complex webs of energy on stage between actors and audience, dissolving barriers and boundaries constructed by old ways of seeing

---

[12] Taken from edited extracts from a paper written by Joseph Bearwalker Wilson in 1978: http://stason.org/TULAR/new-age/shamanism, 1995.
[13] Black: 1987: 22.

and therefore, introducing us to a shamanic concept of 'one' rather than 'separate'.

3. Playing the Exchange

What creates the audience/performer dynamic? How does an actor negotiate the site of energy exchange between breathing bodies in various stages of consciousness? This dynamic lies at the core of the act of theatre. Investigating the relationship between the actor and the audience revealed an enormous gulf, or space wherein seemingly much happens. However, this gulf has not been addressed in current actor training techniques.

The space between the audience and actor is unrehearsed, compared to the usual four to six weeks the actors have spent rehearsing with and to only each other and the director. Playing with the 'metaphysics' or 'ethers' that create the unseen energy medium between actor and audience is an area left to the actor to determine on opening night, and often left out of the actor's conscious tool kit.

I believe theatre is an art form where thought forms attach to performing bodies and can affect the bodies of those watching. These thought forms are almost tangible purveyors of consciousness emitted from the actor consciously and unconsciously. Depending on the sensitivity of the receiver they are picked up consciously or unconsciously. When performing, actors are consciously or unconsciously working with subtle energy bodies emitting from the audience and from the bodies of their fellow actors. These energies can form an almost palpable etheric web, linking the actors and audience together in the same physical space.

Today, the work of renowned Japanese scientist Masaru Emoto contributes significantly to the investigations in the existence and power of thought forms. Emoto's work, based on the fact that the human body is 70-90 percent water (depending on age), establishes through the use of photography that a prayer, words, thoughts or music can all affect considerable transformations on the crystals of water. For example, he would take a photograph of a water crystal and then tape the word 'love' or 'thank you' to a bottle of the same water. He would then photograph the water crystals from the bottle. Then Emoto would tape negative words such as 'I hate you' onto the bottle and photograph the water crystals again. The water receiving the positive messages created beautiful clear crystals, whereas the water receiving the negative words failed to form crystals and generally formed disturbing images. The results are profound and can be found in his book *The Hidden Messages in Water*. Of course the message to me is that the power of thought and intention is more profound than any amount of purely physical training and that it is surely time to combine these elements into contemporary actor training.

The way we train actors affects their ability to reflect the many dimensions of our humanity and potential back to us. This approach to actor training is asking more of the actor, one of 'response-ability': to connect with the audience and to enter into the space of the audience as the audience opens up to the space of the theatre. What is extraordinary about connecting on the inner levels is that it bypasses the actor's occupation with the mental and external worlds. Actors who have developed their inner energies have the possibility to 'consciously' connect with the energies of the audience, and to connect straight through to the deeper states of the being.

> Theatre – through the actor's technique, his art in which the living organism strives for higher motives – provides an opportunity for what could be called integration, the discarding of masks, the revealing of the real substance: a totality of physical and mental reactions. This opportunity must be treated in a disciplined manner, with a full awareness of the responsibilities it involves. Here we can see the theatre's therapeutic function for people in our present day civilization. It is true that the actor accomplishes this act, but he can only do so through an encounter with the spectator – intimately, visibly, not hiding behind a cameraman, wardrobe mistress, stage designer or make-up girl – in direct confrontation with him, and somehow "instead of" him. The actor's act – discarding half measures, revealing, opening up, emerging from himself as opposed to closing up –

is an invitation to the spectator. This act could be compared to an act of the most deeply rooted, genuine love between two human beings – this is just a comparison since we can only refer to this "emergence from oneself" through analogy. This act, paradoxical and borderline, we call a total act. In our opinion it epitomizes the actor's deepest calling.[14]

---

[14] Grotowski 1968: 211.

CHAPTER ONE

Setting the Stage

The creative state of the actor is a complex notion. It carries with it not only the challenge to drop the mask of the socialized being, but also serves as an opening to the many 'forces' within. An actor who recognizes the entrance to her more 'unconscious' states is in a more powerful position in terms of accessing her creative energies than one who is merely focusing on the known 'conscious' state.

Stanislavsky and Chekhov clearly recognized the value of tapping into the deeper aspects of self, beyond the physical and emotional. They both pioneered entry into the spiritual/metaphysical worlds beyond the known physical, emotional and mental by identifying such concepts as the 'Higher I', Prana, Radiation, Meditation and Yoga for use in actor training. "The actors were encouraged to communicate via 'radiation', sending and receiving arrows of intention, attempting to silently communicate their thoughts"[1].

When people are trained for a profession, they are often trained away from natural instincts, intuitions, feelings and dream like states – unless of course they are artists! If I am training for a career in sports, the military, sales, science, trades or any other number of professions other than artistic, I will be trained to respond to the world from my mind and muscles rather than my soul, heart or gut. This is not to say that everyone who is not an artist does not feel from the heart and soul, rather the majority of people have learned a life long habit of

---

[1] Gordon 1981: 38.

steering away from intuition and varying sensitive inner dimensions. In contrast, the artist must seek these places that everyone else has moved away from, and often bears the brunt of being looked upon as having chosen a lesser or weaker career, sometimes even seen as 'soft' compared to the harsher light of seemingly more practical contributions to the society such as building, banking, law and medicine. The actor has no other tool than her body therefore it is vital that she takes on the exploration of that land as Galileo did the stars.

Constantin Stanislavsky (1863-1938)

Constantin Stanislavsky is perhaps best known for developing a technique of acting he initially called 'Spiritual Realism.' Once it transferred to the United States via Lee Strasberg and Stella Adler, it became known as 'method acting' or the 'System.' Variations of his System are still taught in most acting schools today. Identifying the main difference between "the art of the actor and all other arts as the Mastery of inspiration"[2], Stanislavsky set out to discover the meaning of inspiration by attempting to identify the elements that would help the actor to "find a conscious path to unconscious creativeness".[3]

He identified tension as a key impediment to the actor and developed many exercises and frameworks to teach the actor how to become free of these tensions. In any creative state an actor must have a fully free body, entirely empty of the various tensions which unconsciously take hold of her when she is on the stage.[4] "The very best that can happen is to have the actor completely carried away by the play. Then regardless of his own will he lives the part, it all moves of its own accord, subconsciously and intuitively".[5]

---

[2] Stanislavsky 1962: 571.
[3] Ibid.
[4] Muscular tension absorbs an enormous amount of inner energy and therefore cripples the actor from achieving the highest truth on stage. If the actor can develop in himself the habit of freeing the body from superfluous tensions then he removes one of the most substantial blocks to creativity (Stanislavsky 1980: 95-111).
[5] Stanislavsky 1948: 13.

Stanislavsky developed a series of relaxation exercises, which he tested while acting on stage. This series of experiments, while confirming that relaxation had an important part to play in an actor's technique, actually led him deeper into the psyche or consciousness of the actor, resulting finally in the first principle of his technique: "I AM". This means I exist, I live, I feel and I think in the same way as the character I'm presenting on stage. "I AM" is the result of the desire of truth.

Interestingly, "I AM" is also the key phrase of the Theosophy[6] movement which, under the leadership of Madam Helena Blavatsky rose as a powerful spiritual influence at the same time Stanislavsky was developing his actor training techniques.[7]

The connection between the rise of Theosophy, the knowledge of Eastern religious practice, and Stanislavsky's acting System becomes clearer when we discover that not only Nicholas Roerich was a great Russian artist who designed costumes and sets for Stanislavsky,[8] he was also a leading theosophist and he and his wife Helena founded the Agni Yoga Society in 1920.[9] We also discover Stanislavsky was an ardent student of yoga literature, and many passages from the books by Yogi Ramachakara, such as *Hatha Yoga or the Yogi philosophy of physical well-being and The Science of Breath,* are to be found copied in his handwriting onto pages of his rehearsal notes. Certainly there were many influences of the time having an affect on Stanislavsky's search for 'truth' in the craft of acting. However, his deep and continuous interest in the idea of Prana and the yogic and theosophical philosophies related to it appears to stand out. In his

---

[6] The Theosophical Society is a worldwide association dedicated to practical realisation of the oneness of all life and to independent spiritual search. It was founded in New York City in 1875 by Helena P. Blavatsky, Henry S.Olcott, William Q. Judge and others. Blavatsky (1831-1891) is the primary force behind the modern theosophical movement.

[7] Blavatsky addressed the question "What is a theosophist?" and replied "one need not necessarily recognize the existence of any special God or a deity. One need but worship the spirit of living nature, and try to identify oneself with it" (The Theosophist 1879: 6).

[8] Roerich, The Life & Art of a Russian Master 1989: 101.

[9] Ibid. 107, 108.

book on the Stanislavsky Technique,[10] Mel Gordon attributes the very founding of Stanislavsky's System to his nine-year relationship with Leopold Sulerzhitsky. Sulerzhitsky was well versed in Eastern-influenced religious practices, informing Stanislavsky about yoga, meditation and the nature of Prana, "a Hindu concept of the invisible life force that streams through all living things".[11]

Stanislavsky immediately saw the parallel between Prana and the Creative State of Mind. Stanislavsky, in particular, embraced yogic philosophy in an attempt to answer the problem of what he perceived to be a dislocation between the actor's body and soul.[12]

As a result of his strong relationship with Leopold Sulerzhitsky, Stanislavsky saw the links between ideas of vitality, breath and consciousness, realizing that the actor would not grasp the concepts of Relaxation, Attention and Imagination without going to the disciplines of yoga and philosophy, bodies of knowledge containing exercises and approaches to higher awareness that are thousands of years old. "Together, Stanislavsky and Sulerzhitsky laid down these basic building blocks of the System".[13]

The first production to use these acting techniques, as taught by Stanislavsky and Sulerzhitsky, was *A Month in the Country* (1909) by Ivan S. Turgenev, which proved the method so successful it became part of the Moscow Art Theatre's training. Sulerzhitsky also taught the actors exercises of 'radiating the soul,' yoga and meditation, dreaming of the day when "the actor's pure soul could connect directly with the spectator's".[14] When Lee Strasberg and Stella Adler adopted Stanislavsky's 'System' in the 1930s, it seemed that the entirety of "Spiritual Realism" was lost and the 'Method' was constructed. The important group processes and the 'spiritual' training exercises were not adopted as part of the 'Method'. Rather the psychological bent of the time pervaded Stanislavsky's System

---

[10] Gordon 1988: 33.
[11] Ibid. 31.
[12] "In this spiritual and physical disclocation between the body and soul that actors experience." *My Life in Art* 1962: 374 -5.
[13] Gordon 1981: 34.
[14] Gordon 1981: 38.

and the spiritual aspect was forgotten. In an interview with Charles Marowitz, Robert Lewis talked about the 'Method' and the fact that directors like Harold Clurman and Lee Strasberg were only interested in psychology, people's feelings and relationships. Lewis goes on to criticize those directors and the Actors' Studio for their very limited definition of truth, which revolved only around the actors' emotions. "It seems to me that Method has crippled more actors than it ever helped".[15]

The consequence for the Method actor was on one hand a greater depth on the emotional scale and on the other hand a further loss of the sacred and spiritual. Charles Marowitz states: "You have to indict all of the people who put into practice only one portion of it (the Method)…they got stuck in the thirties…you know they're still doing their emotional memories and private moments and sense memory and all the rest of that stuff, and here we are in the eighties, a half-century later. Harold (Clurman) felt that Lee Strasberg had "ghettoized" the American actor".[16]

Stanislavsky and Sulerzhitsky spent many years creating a system of acting, which quite clearly drew much of its inspiration from Eastern forms of spirituality and philosophy. Sulerzhitsky trained the actors initially (over a period of two to three years) on a large plot of land by the Black Sea (purchased by Stanislavsky). This experience instilled a connection to nature within the actors as well as their daily meditations and yoga practice.[17]

For some reason known only to Stanislavsky, the obvious influence of Eastern religious and spiritual teachings and Theosophy has not been clearly acknowledged by him in the construction of his acting techniques. Perhaps they were not acceptable forms of belief or knowledge at the time. Although Stanislavsky referred to the word 'spirit' almost constantly in his writing, there are very few references to what he means by this word.

---

[15] Robert Lewis in interview 1985 (Marowitz 1986: 76).
[16] Lewis in Marowitz 1986: 79.
[17] Stanislavsky 1962: 538, 539.

In his recent article in *Theatre Survey* (May 2006,) *Stanislavsky and Ramacharaka: The Influence of Yoga and Turn-Of-The-Century Occultism on the System*, Andrew White explores in depth the 'spiritual crisis' of Europe in the mid 1800's and the profound affect of Yoga and Indian spirituality on many including Stanislavsky. White writes: "Stanislavsky drew on Yogic practices to enhance concentration on the stage as early as 1906 and cites many examples of the use of spiritual exercises including yoga by the members of the First Studio". [18]

In the same article White quotes Vera Soloviova, a member of the First Studio of the Moscow Art Theatre, who states:

> We worked a great deal on concentration. It was called "To get into the circle." We imagined a circle around us and sent "prana" rays of communion into the space and to each other. Stanislavsky said "send the prana there – I want to reach through the tip of my finger – to God – to the sky- or, later on, my partner. I believe in my inner energy and I give it out- I spread it. [19]

It is clear from the recent research by White that Stanislavsky and the Moscow Art Theatre Actors were deeply engaged in the exploration of 'prana', breath, yoga postures, breathing rhythms and energy radiation. As White's article covers much of this, as well as postulating theories as to why this aspect has not been included in the version we have today of Stanislavsky's technique, I will not go further into the mounting evidence of Stanislavsky's use of yogic philosophy and exercises in the development of his actor training system. The recognition and development of the spiritual within actor training continued with Stanislavsky's brilliant pupil and nephew of Anton Chekhov,[20] Michael Chekhov.

---

[18] White *Theatre Survey* 47: 1. 2006: 78.
[19] Cited in White's article 2006: 79, *Paul Gray The Reality of Doing: Interviews with Vera Soloviova, Stella Adler and Sanford Meisner* in *Stanislavski and America* 1964.
[20] Stanislavsky directed Anton Chekhov's *The Seagull* to acclaim. For the Moscow Art Theatre, Chekhov's well known plays include *Uncle Vanya, The Cherry Orchard* and *The Three Sisters*.

Michael Chekhov (1891-1955)

Michael Chekhov joined the First Studio of the Moscow Art Theatre in 1912. The First Studio, under the leadership of Sulerzhitsky, was set up by Stanislavsky as a site of experimentation and actor training Here he developed under the influences of Stanislavsky, Sulerzhitsky and Yevgeny Vakhtangov.[21] However, his breakthrough as an actor and his development of actor training techniques occurred during his period of exile in Berlin while playing the role as 'Skid', a clown in *Artisten* directed by Max Reinhardt.[22] It was during a performance of *Artisten* that Chekhov first experienced a connection with 'higher' consciousness.

> As one part of Chekhov's consciousness watched and gave commands to the character, another part of his consciousness performed as the character.[23]

[handwritten margin note: See DAMASIOS consciousness problem]

This experience of two separate "I's", the lower and the higher, as different levels of consciousness at work within the individual, catalyzed Chekhov's ideas about acting. He realized that the 'Higher I' was the part of the self that should be engaged, while the 'Lower I' drove the ego and passions, usually resulting in over acting and perhaps melodrama.

The challenge was for Chekhov to identify and develop these two separate 'I's' through his actor training methods. How does one develop the "Higher I" and what is that level of consciousness? He explored alternative approaches in his quest to find a way to train the actor to engage in this other level of consciousness.

Chekhov was deeply inspired by Rudolf Steiner,[24] the founder of Anthroposophy, and used Steiner's System of Eurythmy as a part of

---

[21] One of Stanislavsky's renowned students who eventually disagreed with Stanislavsky's approach, supporting that of Meyerhold.

[22] After learning of his impending arrest in Moscow for his idealist, non Marxist beliefs, Chekhov fled with his wife to Berlin for 7 years from 1928 to 1935. (Black 1987: 21).

[23] Black 1987: 22.

[24] Steiner's most lasting and significant influence has been in the field of education. In 1913 at Dornach, near Basel, Switzerland, Steiner built his Goetheanum, "school of spiritual science". This would be a forerunner of the Steiner or Waldorf schools.

his own acting system. The Austrian-born Rudolf Steiner (1861-1925) was the head of the German *Theosophical* Society from 1902 until 1912, at which time he broke away and formed the Anthroposophical Society. Steiner was also concerned with the arts and was a key thinker in the revolution of consciousness taking place at the turn of the century.

> Rudolf Steiner was looking for an art that would lift the veil between the spiritual and material dimensions of life; an art that would make the language of the spiritual world visible. His explorations brought him to the utterances of the human being; speaking and singing. As described in "About Eurythmy," human sound is a bridge between the two dimensions of life, inner and outer, spiritual and material. Eurythmy reveals the deeper origins of life through the embodiment of the spiritual forces that live within human speaking and singing.[25]

Eurythmy, also termed the science of visible speech, consisted of spiritual dances attempting to transform sound and color into movement. The following is an excerpt from one of Steiner's lectures on Eurythmy;

> The etheric body never uses the mouth as the vehicle of speech, but invariably makes use of the limb-System. And it is those movements made by the etheric body during speech which are transferred into the physical body. Of course you can, if you choose, speak quite without gesture, even going so far as to stand rigidly still with your hands in your pockets; but in that case your etheric body will gesticulate all the more vigorously, sheerly out of protest! Thus you can see how, in very truth, Eurythmy is drawn out of the human organisation in just as natural a way as speech itself.[26]

---

[25] Taken from website http://www.eurythmy.org/history1.htm.
[26] Rudolph Steiner, lecture given in Penmaenmawr, Wales on August 26th, 1923. http://wn.rsarchive.org/Eurhythmy/19230826p01.html.

As the ideas and writings of Madam Blavatsky, Annie Besant and A.E. Powell were circulating Europe, it is likely Steiner drew on these Theosophical writings about the Etheric Body as inspiration for his use of the term 'etheric body'. A.E. Powell's book, *The Etheric Double* was a compilation from forty main works on the Etheric Body published between 1897 and 1921.

Chekhov introduced Eurythmy in his teaching method to make actors aware of the qualities of speech, citing that vowels are more intimate and suitable for expressing cantabile, spiritual themes and intimate experiences whereas consonants are more dramatic and earthy.[27] It should be noted that Chekhov was also a "strong believer in yoga and felt that there was something in the practice of yoga that would be of great use to the actor. He experimented with ways to use it in rehearsals and performances".[28] Although Chekhov used Eurhythmy in his actor training exercises and certainly embodied the philosophy of Anthroposophy in his work, he does not mention specific Steiner exercises in his books.

Franc Chamberlain[29] provides a very good insight to this quandary in his article *Michael Chekhov: Pedagogy, Spirituality, and the Occult.* "Since this is a summary of his life's work and it includes no specific instruction in Eurythmy it seems reasonable to conclude that Chekhov didn't consider it essential to discuss the relationship of Eurythmy to his technique".[30]

One of Chekhov's techniques for actors is a method to refine the imagination to the extent that the actor can incorporate the character into her state of mind. The actor questions the image of the character in her mind's eye as she would a friend. Chekhov maintains that answers will be forthcoming if the imagination is flexible and courageous. Instead of guessing what the character's response might

---

[27] Chekhov 1991: 75.
[28] Black 1987: 7.
[29] Franc Chamberlain is a writer, performer and visual artist. He was the editor of *Contemporary Theatre Review and Contemporary Theatre Studies* from 1991-2000 and is currently the editor of two book series: *Routledge Performance Practitioners* and *Routledge Companions to Theatre Practitioners.*
[30] *Toronto Slavic Quarterly* (TSQ) volume 4. University of Toronto.

be to a given situation or circumstance, the actor observes the character responding to that situation. ᒪ.ℓ ᔆⲦⲦⲦⲤ⳿

Absolute trust comes as a result of constant use and total belief in this method. The essence of this technique is that the image rehearses for the actor. Asking leading questions is the means by which the actor drives the image, placing the actor's body into the imaginary body. Lifting the imaginary arm with the real, (e.g., the character's arm is long and lean) the actor rehearses with this new arm until it is long and lean, and then continues with the rest of her body. As the actor incorporates the imaginary body she will also establish the 'centre' of the character's body.

The centre is described by Chekhov as the 'watchtower'[31] of the body, once the actor connects with the centre of the character, all else will fall into place. Two key aspects of Chekhov's work are the use of imagination and the notion of the "Higher I". By use of imagination, the actor is encouraged through intense focus to imagine the character, internally and externally, and to ask questions of the character. This key concept replaced Stanislavsky's Emotion Memory or Recall and introduced the actor to the world beyond the conscious.

Most creative visualization techniques today draw on similar exercises, e.g., seeing yourself as successful in your mind. The use of Eurythmy by Chekhov engaged the actor's imagination past the senses into the realms of 'radiation'[32] and focused energy work; "Marrying the inner truth and emotional depth of Stanislavsky's System with the beauty and spiritual impact of Steiner's work became Chekhov's obsessive quest".[33]

The second key aspect of Chekhov's work, the "Higher I," potentially takes the actor into realms of a spiritual 'at oneness' with her part and ideally the audience. Listening to the 'voice' speaking

---

[31] Chekhov 1991: 102.
[32] A further development of the work on radiation initiated by Sulerzhitsky and Stanislavsky.
[33] Gordon 1988: 16.

from the audience was an important part of the training. The work of Michael Chekhov always had at its foundation the search for a greater level of communion with the audience.[34] Have we lost this notion today?

Most importantly, in Chekhov's technique the use of logical reason is always inferior to the use of imagination.[35] In his address to the Drama Society of Hollywood in 1955 Chekhov stated; "Deep within ourselves are buried tremendous creative powers and abilities. But they remain unused so long as we deny them….They lie dormant because we do not open the doors to our hidden vaults and fearlessly bring them to the surface".[36]

Antonin Artaud (1896-1948)

Along with Stanislavsky and Michael Chekhov, Antonin Artaud worked to bring consciousness of soul and spirit back to the theatre. Perhaps Artaud's most insightful writing on this matter is the following from his book, *The Theatre and its Double*:

> The question then, for the theater, is to create a metaphysics of speech, gesture, and expression…. But all this can be of no use unless behind this effort there is some kind of real metaphysical inclination, an appeal to certain un-habitual ideas, which by their very nature cannot be limited or even formally depicted. These ideas which touch on Creation, Becoming and Chaos, are all of a cosmic order and furnish a primary notion of a domain from which the theatre is entirely alien.[37]

The terms 'cosmic order' and 'metaphysical inclinations' suggest a movement of forces seemingly untapped by the theatre of his time.

---

[34] Chekhov 1991: xvi.
[35] Black 1987: 97.
[36] Chekhov 1953: 17.
[37] Artaud 1994: 90-91.

Artaud was concerned by the lack of connection to soul and saw this as a huge setback for the actor. "Belief in the soul's flowing substantiality is essential to the actor's craft...To know there is a physical outlet for the soul permits him to journey down into that soul."[38]

Peter Brook writes that Artaud "...was always speaking of a complete way of life, of a theatre in which the activity of the actor and the activity of the spectator were driven by the same desperate need."[39] I wonder if the idea of audience and actors sharing the same desperate need is at work today but perhaps a search for who we are and a desire for meditation and reflection on our human state constitute this. Brook also states "...the theatre is based on a particular human characteristic, which is the need at times to be in a new intimate relationship with one's fellow men".[40] He suggests that theatre is capable of a dynamic between both audience and actors, which invites an intimate experience not available elsewhere. The sharing of the space and the altering of the space are realms into which both the actor and spectator step when they arrive at the site of theatre. Mark Fortier,[41] a specialist in Shakespeare, contemporary theatre and cultural studies comments, "Derrida concludes that no theatre can be what Artaud proposes" simply because he believes that "Western theatre has been separated form the forces of its essence".[42] Have the ideas of 'gods' and 'sacred' been dropped from Western theatre rendering it immobile and disconnected from the original reasons for its existence? Is Derrida meaning more specifically, a loss of interconnectedness between ourselves and each other, between our body and soul and if so, where is theatre's place in this?

Theatre involves many transactions between actors and audience – a sense of an otherness within us all which is connected through the act of theatre inside the shared space. Iben Nagel Rasmussen from Odin

---

[38] Artaud 1997: 90.
[39] Brook 1990: 6.
[40] Brook 1989: 147.
[41] Currently director of the School of English and Theatre Studies at the University of Guelph, Ontario, Canada.
[42] Fortier 1997: 44.

Teatret observes "Otherness is our meeting place"[43] suggesting that within the act of theatre there is a site where a part of our deeper or inner self can connect with each other. 'Otherness' brings with it a concept of another part of us, an inner part, unknown and known, recognizable intuitively and through the senses, a metaphysical attachment to the known self. The actor's awareness of these engaging metaphysical energies present in the shared space has yet to be clarified by present Western training techniques. However, Jerzy Grotowski was one of several practitioners who, with his actors, explored the metaphysics of this shared space.

Jerzy Grotowski (1933-1999)

Although on a nearly religious path of actor training, Grotowski's approach was less embracing of the inner dimensions, and more focused on the act of ritual than either Stanislavsky or Chekhov. In his own words, he defines the 'holy actor' as one "who, through his art, climbs upon the stake and performs an act of self sacrifice".[44] Grotowski began to think in terms of "another hitherto unknown form of art beyond the traditional division of onlooker and active person creator and recipient"[45] as his paratheatrical work took participants from cities and brought them to remote areas to work with his actors, performing actions that involved discovering and revealing hidden personal themes. "The actor makes a complete gift of himself. This is a technique of the 'trance' and of the integration of all the actor's psychic and bodily powers which emerge from the most intimate layers of his being and his instinct, springing forth in a sort of 'translumination'".[46] Many of the physical actions, running through the forest at night, sudden immersion in water, dances around fire, group chanting, etc., are very like those in initiation rites.

---

[43] Barba 1986: 54.
[44] Grotowski: 1984: 43.
[45] Mitter 1995: 102.
[46] Grotowski 1968: 15.

Why was Grotowski drawn to these exercises for his actors? The International Research Theatre Group KISS[47] based in Holland also explored similar rituals in the search for material and actor training methods. For example, one such ritual in preparation for a 24-hour show based on Dante's *Divine Comedy* involved actors spending a 24-hour period, with no break, building and worshipping effigies of the seven deadly sins. This ritual served to alter the actors' waking state of perception and creativity, which often resulted in a dream-like trance state where they drew on resources deep within that had previously been untapped. Grotowski was searching for a state of the actor that was her 'true' state; the state that exists past the roles, identities and masks created by our cultures. According to Shomit Mitter, "It is the objective of Grotowski's theatre to destroy social roles so that actor and spectator alike can achieve a true self-realization",[48] whereas the KISS actors entered into altered states in order to access and draw on their creativity. "We are concerned with the spectator who has genuine spiritual needs and who really wishes, through confrontation, to analyse himself".[49] If certain boundaries of culture, self and other were transcended as a result of this training, this was an added aspect and often not identified as such at the time.

Grotowski's style may be described as one of isolation and control, as demonstrated in many of the Oriental performing arts. Richard Schechner in his book *Between Theatre & Anthropology* discusses Grotowski's work with concern for the actor who, after this training, becomes "disenabled".[50] Grotowski did not leave the actor a road map home after the training. As Schechner observes, "People are drawn very deeply into highly personal work – into the 'breakdown' phase of the workshop, or the 'separation/ordeal' phase of initiation – but they are not then 'reconstructed'".[51]

---

[47] International Research Theatre Group KISS was founded by Jean-Pierre Voos in 1972 and disbanded in 1984 after successful tours throughout Europe, Australia and the U.S.
[48] Mitter 1992: 82.
[49] Grotowski 1975: 40.
[50] Schechner 1989: 255.
[51] Ibid.

In her article "Action", Lisa Wolford notes the observation made by Peter Brook in 1987 that Grotowski is looking for "...something which existed in the past but has been forgotten over the centuries. That is that one of the vehicles, which allows humanity to have access to another level of perception is to be found in the art of the performer".[52] Wolford's quote brings light to Grotowski's later work and his concern with performance as a means to give form and structure to the inner search, likening the process to that of certain orders of monks who used the making of music or the making of liqueurs to provide a practical structure and focus for their inner development. Some of his later work from 1986 on, developed at Grotowski's Work Centre, Pondetera, Italy, focused on "Art as Vehicle", the development of performance structures around songs from African and Afro-Caribbean lines of tradition. The performance structure functioned as an objective support that assisted the actor in what Grotowski terms an "itinerary in verticality"[53] involving a movement from coarser earthly forms to finer more subtle energy forms.

Grotowski's concept of verticality is not dissimilar to how the chakras work and the nature of the accompanying energy bodies to each chakra. The seven key chakras move from coarser energy at the root to finer energy at the crown. An actor working with the chakras would certainly be experiencing progressions through detectably different levels and grades of energy.

Grotowski wanted to investigate the innate physical power known in the Hindu tradition as 'kundalini,' the sleeping energy at the base of the spine. He believed that the awakened state was necessary both in life and in art. Grotowski also recognised the enormous potential of theatre to alter the audience's states of consciousness, awareness and perception. He saw theatre as transformative for both actor and audience: "If the actor, by setting himself a challenge publicly challenges others...reveals himself by casting off his everyday mask,

---

[52] Wolford "Action", in *The Drama Review,* Winter 1996: 135.
[53] Lendra 1995: 153.

he makes it possible for the spectator to undertake a similar process of self-penetration".[54]

Through intensive questioning of the actors about their true selves, Grotowski placed the actors into self-reflective modes of awareness beyond an everyday self-knowledge. Sometimes using song as a vehicle of expression, he would suggest "sing your name…evoke this Joseph. Who is he this stranger?[55] Known for his somewhat ruthless approach towards pushing the actor beyond his limits, he created many ritual tasks for the actor involving grueling physical challenges that would serve to alter the actor's waking senses in a very real way.

James Waites,[56] in an article on Grotowski in *RealTime,*[57] related details of being used as a human plough and made to stand in freezing water in a large tub while standing on pineapple tops. Waites also was repeatedly hit by a woman trying to goad him into a fight in which he refused to engage (Waites had been selected for a Grotowski workshop in Armidale, New South Wales, Australia). These were all tests of endurance and very punishing ways to take the actor into altered states of reality.

When Grotowski asked, "In what conditions is it possible to achieve interhuman fullness?"[58] it seems strange that he did not consider the effects of meditation, Eastern religious practices and shamanism, as these approaches and exercises have been developed for thousands of years to assist the individual in developing 'interhuman fullness', a higher state, altered state or a 'oneness' with the forces or 'god.' Grotowski was concerned with developing the actor's state into "the one who watches and the one who acts…the recipient and the creator",[59] a state not unlike Chekhov's observation of the 'Higher I' and the 'Lower I'.

---

[54] Grotowski 1969: 34.
[55] Ibid. 170.
[56] A Sydney journalist and theatre critic.
[57] A Sydney arts magazine, editor Keith Gallasch. April-May 1999: 7.
[58] Schechner 1989: 254.
[59] Ibid.

Although some performance theories today, particularly in dance,(see Barbara Sellers-Young *Breathing, Movement, Exploration*, Janet Adler *Offering from the Conscious Body: The Discipline of Authentic Movement*, Andrea Olsen *A Guide to Experiential Anatomy*), would argue that there is no division between body and mind, my experiences of meditation, yoga and contemporary shamanic practice have placed my awareness in at least two places, one as the observer, always present, and one within the 'feeling body.' This is a problematic description but I hope a richer sense of what this aspect of the body might be called becomes clearer in the following chapters.

Grotowski's focus on the self of the actor rather than the identity of the character distinguished his work from Chekhov and Stanislavsky. The fact that his work over the past twenty years developed to a point where the audience was no longer required, or even desirable, begs the debate as to whether this was 'theatre' or 'therapy.' This debate I will leave for another time and which, I believe, Rustom Bharucha in His book *Theatre and the World*,[60] in a chapter entitled 'Goodbye Grotowski', deals with well. However, Grotowski's searching for this 'enlightened' state is reminiscent of a spiritual disciple. Citing no 'god' in particular as the ideal or example, the actor went forward into the unknown regions with no aid from the ancient structures developed for such journeys. As a result, no specific outcome was outlined as a part of the art form, and Grotowski's actor was left somewhere on the path of the inner self. When commenting on the difficulty of leaving thought behind and just 'being,' Grotowski stated in his address to the Kosciuszko Foundation in 1979, "The tree is our teacher. It does not ask itself such questions".[61] Grotowski was influenced by Kathakali training and Hatha Yoga,[62] yet he only borrowed specific physical exercises and not the informing spirituality behind the practice.

The legacies of Stanislavsky, Chekhov, Artaud and Grotowski live on in our work today. They are more recently joined by practitioners

---

[60] Bharucha 1993: 42 -53.
[61] Mitter 1992: 88.
[62] Schechner 1989: 227, 8.

and theorists such as Brook, Schechner, Boal, Barba, Bogart, Suzuki, Fitzmaurice and many others. The experimenting, investigating, researching and rehearsing go on as we search for revelation through theatre via our actors.

Performance, Ritual, Altered States and Acting

> In the ritual, one has to have participants who are invisible and can actually produce a result that is unexpected. And because we take the risk or the initiative of putting a request to the spirits to intervene in our affairs, their coming turns our activity (ceremony) into a ritual...The gods themselves will not enact the ritual without us...So Spirit is our channel through which every gap in life can be filled.[63]

Invisible presence is not a concept embraced in the West outside the established church. For performers to be acknowledging the invisible presence of 'god-like' forces in our theatre, some fairly large areas of actor training and rehearsal formulae need to be addressed. When considering the rituals that might be carried out by actors in our Western theatre before a performance, it is evident there are very few that involve the 'sacred' or 'spiritual'. One might well ask at what point in history was Western theatre 'connected' to the force of its essence. In his book *Between Theatre & Anthropology,* Schechner talks about the significance of ritual in both rehearsal and preparation. "Immediately before going on stage, most performers engage in some ritual. The Noh actor contemplates his mask; Jatra performers in Bengal worship the gods of the performance, Stanislavsky advised 30 seconds of silent concentration".[64] Although Eastern, Western and indigenous performers all engage in some aspect of ritual, it appears the Western actor rarely acknowledges the presence of a 'god,' or higher self when acting out the ritual. There are many ways to define ritual and one was that of Malidoma in the earlier quote. For a broader understanding of ritual in the

---

[63] Malidoma 1993: 127.
[64] Schechner 1989: 105.

performative sense, it is interesting to compare Richard Schechner's five different viewpoints on ritual stated in his introduction to Victor Turner's book *The Anthropology of Performance* with Turner's definitions on the subject. Schechner considers ritual to be:

1) As part of the evolutionary development of organisms including, but not limited to, the development of the brain;
2) As a structure, something with formal qualities and relationships;
3) As a performance process, a dynamic System or action;
4) As experience, as what a person individually or as part of a collective feels;
5) As a set of operations in human social and religious life.[65]

Turner describes ritual as 'transformative' as "the performance of a complex sequence of symbolic acts"[66]. He is using 'transformative' to describe a movement that will move the performer to a new status and social position (within the tribe). Turner further suggests that ritual is transformative as it transforms personal and social life crises such as "birth, initiation, marriage, death, into occasions where symbols and values representing the unity and continuity of the total Group"[67] are celebrated and reanimated.

Meyer Fortes[68] defined ritual as "a procedure for prehending the occult".[69] He saw ritual as a way of humankind attempting to connect to or handle seemingly unmanageable powers. Both Turner and Fortes seem to support the notion that rituals are involved with forces beyond our knowing and seeing, an attempt to come to an understanding of the meaning of the greater events in life such as birth and death.

This to me is immediately applicable to theatre and certainly my experience of theatre in Europe in 1978 – 1980 came close to this

---

[65] Schechner in Turner 1986: 10.
[66] Schechner in Turner 1986: 10.
[67] Ibid. 157.
[68] William Wyse Professor of Anthropology and Archeology, Cambridge University.
[69] Turner 1986: 158.

idea of ritual. As a member of the International Theatre Research Group KISS, I experienced altered states during the training and performances. I also observed Pina Baush's work in nearby Wuppertal, Germany once a month and was again transformed and altered by her work. Bausch is the artistic director and choreographer of the "Tanztheatre Wuppertal Pina Bausch" company, based in Wuppertal and a leading influence in Tanztheatre (dance theatre). However, on returning to Australia and becoming involved with theatre as a street performer, performance artist, student and eventually, director, I was unable to discover where this kind of theatre might exist. I realize now that it was the transformative, sacred and ritualized aspects of the theatre I had been engaged with in Holland and witnessing in Wuppertal that I was searching for in Australia.

This leads me to ask the same question Schechner asks, have we lost the 'sacred' in our performance because it has become a 'product?' "When the consumer audience comes in, the 'spiritual powers depart".[70] He writes about the focus within a sacred performance of the Yaqui Deer Dance, which is intrinsically designed and performed for a very specific audience;[71] the moment it is taken out of this context and performed for non-Indian people, the 'spiritual powers' are removed. "Understand that the spiritual benefits of the song are withdrawn if the song is commercialized".[72] One might say it is the location, intention, purpose and type of audience that defines the nature of the performance.

Many church services could be considered 'sacred' in respect to the common aims of the audience and performers. The purpose could be to come closer to 'god' and to enter a higher state of self through prayer and singing of religious songs. How has our mainstream theatre been removed from these signifiers?

One reason our Western audience comes to the theatre is to witness a story, one they might know or one they're curious to know. They do

---

[70] Schechner 1989: 6.
[71] Ibid. 10.
[72] Ibid. 5.

not usually know the performers or many others in the audience. There is not a defined sacred approach by the performers to the material or any particular approach to the playing stage as a sacred space or a site of exchange between the 'gods' and humans.

Mircea Eliade's work illuminates the idea of an age-long search for meaning where the sacred is an experience where the world means something: "It lives and speaks to the religious person".[73] He connects the idea of 'religious man' to an "infinite series of experiences that could be termed cosmic".[74] Although a 'religious man' to Eliade included anyone who acknowledged a 'god' in their life, this loose definition was still limited to more traditional religions, East and West. However, Eliade's ideas on the sacred move us towards a clearer understanding of constructions of meaning via religion as opposed to the existential dilemma of the non-religious[75]. Within this he suggests that 'the 'irreligious' still behave religiously without being conscious of the fact that they are conditioned by myths, rituals and taboos from religious ceremonies handed down from other eras.[76]

All of this serves to support the premise behind the re-development of the sacred in the theatre, which is the fact that we, as human beings, have constructed our meaning through religious rituals for thousands of years. If theatre is to remain meaningful to us it must reconsider these roots in the light of today's changing views and interpretations of meaningful religious and spiritual experiences. By reclaiming the sacred, theatre can embrace a genuine spirituality involving a connectedness with the forces surrounding us, both earthly and otherwise. By the term 'spiritual', I mean a more shamanic rather than religious approach, one that connects into ideas of altered consciousness, working with the shared etheric energies in the auditorium and integrating notions of 'Higher Self'. If we are to bring the notion of the spiritual back into the theatre, we need to

---

[73] Eliade 1959: 165.
[74] Ibid. 170.
[75] Ibid. 14 -18.
[76] Ibid. 205.

address the training of the representatives, the story tellers and the actors.

The approach to actor training explored in this book is aimed to access the inner spaces and to develop a language and understanding of consciousness in ways that empower, excite and constructively aid the actor in her creation of character and quality of acting. It is clear that these inner spaces of self are difficult to articulate. Each practitioner quoted is searching for a way in, to access the 'hidden vaults'. They all knew that the depths of creativity lay within these places, past consciousness, deep within the self, and difficult to describe in words although the writing of feminist philosopher Hélène Cixous invites us towards these places, 'It is deep in my body, further down, behind thought. Thought comes in front of it and it closes like a door. This does not mean that it does not think, but it thinks differently from our thinking and speech".[77]

Historical traditions of actor training have struggled with the inclusion of techniques for the development of the 'inner space self', while simultaneously searching for a way into those excluded spaces. As an illustration of this, one exercise practiced throughout centuries by many traditional primitive societies is that of listening to inner voices that might appear as spirits, visions or just voices. Much weight was given to the importance of these messages; they often gave guidance to the whole tribe. Even Carl Jung, a leading 'guru' of the science of psychology, discovered an inner voice which he called 'Philemon' and engaged in receiving messages from the realms 'beyond'.

> Philemon and other figures of my fantasies brought home to me the crucial insight that there are things in the psyche which I do not produce, but which produce themselves and have their own life. Philemon represented a force which was not myself. In my fantasies I held conversations with him, and he said things which I had not consciously thought. For I observed clearly that it

---

[77] Cixous 1994: 204.

was he who spoke, not I. Psychologically,
Philemon represented superior insight.[78]

In Jung's view, the psyche is not just a place inside the mind, but a realm or dimension of reality of non-physical character: the realm of Spirit or Dreaming. This is the dimension recognized by Stanislavsky, Chekhov, Artaud and Grotowski as important, if not vital, to the actor's process.

Hopefully, my approach to actor training remains respectful to this search, not attempting to replace these systems but to add to them as a natural act of progression.

---

[78] Jung 1965: 183.

CHAPTER TWO

Body Energy Centres (BECs)

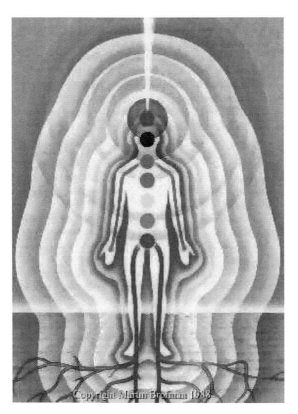

Figure 1. Image compliments of Martin Brofman.[1]

[1] http://www.healer.ch/BMS.html.

The term Body Energy Centre (BEC) describes a place in the body that correlates with what is also known as a chakra. Chakra is a Sanskrit word which has been translated into several meanings, including 'spinning wheel,' 'wheel of light' and 'wheel.' "These seven force-Centres are frequently described in Sanskrit literature, in some of the minor Upanishads, in the Puranas and in Tantric works".[2] The underlying idea behind the concept of the BECs is that our body is not only physical, mental and emotional, but also etheric or made up of energy, and that energy body is responsive to our attention and focus. This concept includes the notions of thought forms, telepathy, radiation and transformation.

How does an actor work with their energy body? The system of BECs has been developed as a tool to assist you in learning about seven key focus points of energy in the body, creation of character, focusing text through a particular Centre, maintaining a healthy neutral body and as a means of exploring your body.

I have chosen not to work directly with the chakras for a myriad of reasons; they are a complex ancient system requiring many years of devotion and are linked to very particular belief systems and structures. Using the BECs will allow you to move freely through your own experience of bodily response with no specific outcome requisites such as evolving into your higher self, awakening the Kundalini or experiencing a blissful connection with 'God'. If you are familiar with chakras, you will see some correspondence between the BECs and the chakras.

There are several different systems of chakras and also many different methods of accessing, opening and exploring these Energy Centres of the Body. Theosophists view the chakras as a mechanism through which communication between the higher, 'etheric' bodies and the physical body occurs. The chakra is represented in Indian Arts, sculptures, yoga and Tantra philosophy of India, and is used to explain spiritual or divine centres in the human body, which can be invoked through yoga to experience heightened experiences and enlightenment of the human life. The idea of chakras has been around

---

[2] Leadbeater 1980: 18.

for a very long time. They were referred to in the ancient literature of the Vedas more than four thousand years ago[3] and elaborated in early writings in Hindu canonical literature around the tenth century, particularly in the writing of Guru Goraknath who set out practical knowledge of the chakras for the benefit of his disciples.[4] According to Ozaniec, the most detailed and comprehensive historical study of the chakras can be found in the *Sat-Cakra-Nirupana* (Description of and Investigation into the Six Bodily Centres), composed in the sixteenth century by Purananda Svami in a larger work entitled *Shri-Tattva-Cintamini.*[5] The chakras have been seen as doors to the inner worlds and, therefore, to inner states of consciousness. As you develop and open each chakra, you open to the level of consciousness that chakra is related to.

The BECs are also openings to inner worlds within the body and to different states of consciousness and awareness. The key difference here between BECs and chakras is that the different states of consciousness and awareness in each Centre are focused on the task of acting and creating a character. For instance, if you are working with the throat chakra you might be intent on opening this chakra to express your voice clearly or to creatively express your feelings. An actor working with the Throat BEC is not only developing the ability to open this Centre but also to close it, to leak it and to use it in the role of a character. This character may have a closed Throat BEC, which through the course of the story his Throat BEC gradually opens so finally he is able to express himself.

However, the BECs differ from the chakras in several ways. The BEC system does not venture into the 'spiritual' potential of the being as chakra work does. It does not follow the clockwise and anti-clockwise movement of the chakras, nor does the concept of 'Kundalini' come into play.

---

[3] Judith 2004: 5.
[4] Ozaniec 1996: 5.
[5] Ozaniec 1995: 7.

The BEC technique uses seven core Centres of the Body;

Figure 2. The seven BECs, starting from the Root at the bottom,
moving to the Crown at the top.[6]

1. Root
2. Belly
3. Solar
4. Heart
5. Throat
6. Mind
7. Crown

Although it is possible and likely that the actor will develop a greater
'spiritual consciousness' through consistent use of this system, this is
not the key function of it. The BEC system has been created
specifically for use as an actor training methodology, to develop a
user-friendly common language in the rehearsal room, and to

---

[6] Diagram by Shanti Portia, Daylesford, Victoria.

facilitate not only the creation of character and voice, but also to provide a safe and easy way to de-role each night after performance. For example, if you are playing Willie Loman in *Death of a Salesman* and have chosen to work with mainly the Heart BEC and the Root BEC, then after the performance you would use the breathing exercise (see page 53 on of this chapter) down through all of the BECs, bringing each one back into balance. Once all Centres are balanced, the character is no longer residing in the muscles and organs, although within the consciousness it is possible that elements of Willie Loman will still exist. When preparing to perform the following night, you will again reconstruct the BECs you are using and the character of Willie Loman will manifest in the body again.

BEC work relies heavily upon the use of breath and concentration in connection with the exploration of varying altered states of awareness within the process of character creation and performing a role. This technique is the development of exercises that locate, develop and enhance the body energies, providing a framework that can offer an imaginative focus on various areas of the body, including physical, mental, emotional and energetic. With a combination of breath and focus of attention, these Centres of the body become enlivened and active, deepening the actor's overall control and use of the body and all that is associated with it.

Just as directors and actor trainers in the past developed exercises to assist the actor, these exercises are geared to expand the potential of the actor's resources and skills for today's world and today's consciousness. For example, Stanislavsky's exercise *Circles of Attention* trains the actor to focus on a small circle around his body, then to expand the circle to include another actor and to continue expanding this circle until it eventually includes the audience. By focusing on these 'circles' an actor could enhance his concentration, expanding and contracting it at will but always staying in the life of the character.

Generally, we can say that the three lower BECs are related to the raw emotions and biological instincts ranging from sexual desire and hunger, into passion, anger, pleasure and joy and other relatively simple emotional states. The four higher BECs are related to higher cognitive states. The Heart BEC is the meeting Centre of the higher and lower selves, relating to empathy and understanding. The Throat BEC is associated with vocal expression, hearing, and the ability to communicate. The Mind BEC deals with discriminative cognition and the ability to understand, the Crown BEC is also related to understanding and comprehension, but also serves as an integrative factor with a connection to the higher self or the universal self.

Here is a brief overview of each Body Centre, its location and key concepts within the consciousness of that Centre. Be mindful that the energy in each Centre extends beyond the physical body both front and back.

Part One Locating the Body Energy Centres

The Body Energy Centres are directly related to the positioning of the seven major chakra centres of the body.

ROOT

Element: Earth

Location: The perineum, the middle point between the anus and the sex organs.

Consciousness:

- Security, survival, and trust.
- Your relationship with money, home, career.
- Ability to be grounded, to be present in the here and now.
- Connection with the earth via the grounding cord, a sense of place in the world.

When you observe the way native people dance with their feet, you will see a 'stomping' of physical energy into the ground, for instance, by Aboriginal, North American Indians and Africans. This action of stomping the feet into the ground stimulates the Root Centre and assists in the connection to earth.

BELLY

Element: Water

Location: Between one to two inches below the belly button.

Consciousness:

- Associated with food and sex.
- What the body wants and needs and what it finds pleasurable.
- Associated with the emotional body and willingness to feel emotions.

Hawaiian dancers engage in a wonderful exercise for the Belly BEC with the Hula dance. This dance fluidly rotates and moves the entire area connected to this Energy Centre, allowing the dancer to engage in the full energy of this Centre.

SOLAR

Element: Fire, the sun.

Location: Solar plexus, behind the diaphragm and stomach.

Consciousness:

- Perceptions concerned with power, control and freedom.
- The ease with which one is able to be oneself — ease of being. Mental activity and the mental body are also associated with this BEC.
- Associated with the level of being often called the personality, or ego.

- This Centre is about personal power, the belief in oneself and the ability to uphold one's beliefs. Sometimes a person with a low sense of self can appear collapsed at this Centre, as though it almost does not exist. In others, who might have an over-developed Solar Centre, you can see that this Centre leads their walk.

A good exercise for awakening this Centre is a wood chopping action with feet shoulder- width apart, knees slightly bent, hands clasped and raised behind the head, bending the knees further, bringing the arms down in a rushing movement towards the floor. At the same time let out a sound, 'ah,' as the hands finish through the legs and the head is completely dropped, a little like the movement of chopping wood.

HEART

Element: Air

Location: Centre of the chest.

Consciousness:

- Ability to love in a broader sense than the romantic idea of love.
- Able to love less conditionally and towards people as a whole.
- Love associated with the Heart BEC is a higher love not based in need or on conditions. (Romantic 'one on one' love is associated more with the Belly BEC, desire, pleasure and procreation.)

A good way to open this Centre is via circular movement of the arms at shoulder level, combining breath with circular arm movement and sending the energy across the chest from the tip of one hand to the tip of the other.

THROAT

Element: Sound

Location: Base of the throat.

Consciousness:

- The aspects of expressing and receiving.
- Communicating what one wants and what one feels.
- Using a form for expressing and bringing to the outside what was within — artistic expression, painting, dancing, and playing music.

The Throat Centre is the 'voice' to all the impulses within, a channel of expression and very important to work with until you feel it is open.

MIND

Element: Ether

Location: Centre of the forehead.

Consciousness:

- Vision, the ability to see beyond, intuition, telepathy and thought forms.
- Sometimes referred to as 'the mind's eye'.

To be in this Centre requires placing your awareness at the midpoint between the forehead and back of the head and between the ears, rather than at the front of the forehead between the eyes.

The Mind and Crown BECs connect us with 'higher' and more universal interpretations of life. The Mind BEC is associated with the brain and when open, thoughts and mental processes are infused with a greater clarity and wisdom.

Exercising this Centre involves creative visualizing, day dreaming, seeing images in the mind's eye and watching them without judgment and embracing the ideas and messages within these.

CROWN

Element: Ether, Astral.

Location: Top of the head.

Consciousness:

- The view from this BEC includes seeing one's self as the single consciousness creating all, and paradoxically connected to all, like a dreamer dreaming a dream and realizing that all that is perceived is just an extension of his own consciousness.
- The opening of this Centre occurs with focus and attention on breath, visualizing a spiral of energy emerging from the top of the head towards the sky and allowing your awareness to follow the breath through that Centre.
- When Michael Chekhov spoke about the 'Higher I', it is very likely he was referring to the energy point beyond the Crown approximately two to fifteen feet above the head where the energy from the Crown meets a higher, wiser aspect of self, or soul.
- It is also from this point of view that one sees events in the physical world as the manifestation of co-creation with others involved in those events. This point of view takes on a responsibility for one's position in the world.

Note:
There is a wealth of information on these Centres as chakras available online, in books, magazines, journals and workshops. For this approach the best information comes from your own body.

THE EXERCISES

The following exercises will assist the actor in establishing a dialogue and a language for the use of these Centres. It is important to work through these Centres from the Root up because opening a Centre by itself without connection to the whole can often result in disconnectedness of that part of the body from the rest of the body.

As you work through these Centres with breath, movement and character, the idea of each Centre as a different place of consciousness becomes established in your body. Often these sites of consciousness are beyond words and are unique to each body. Ideally, you will engage in these exercises, breathing and dancing the BECs daily, for at least two weeks before embarking on the journey of applying this knowledge to the creation of character and the rehearsal. Creating your own images that assist you opening a Body Energy Centre is ideal as we all respond to different stimuli.

For example, one image that helped me to open my Throat Centre:

Lie on your back, relax and focus on your Throat BEC. Imagine a straw entering the centre of the throat, going directly into the windpipe so you can draw air straight into that centre rather than through the nose or mouth. As this becomes easier you can then expand the circle, let go of the straw and breathe directly into the Throat BEC. Remember that the energy in each centre extends past the physical body both front and back.

It is vital for you to know your own energy body state before adapting it to that of the character. For example, if you are not engaging with your own Heart BEC and do not realise that BEC is closed or blocked then it will be more difficult to play a character with an open heart. Clearing your own BECs first (as much as possible) allows for a 'clean slate', a ready body to embrace the nuances of the character.

More importantly, this process allows you to return to a neutral state after the performance by simply breathing down through the BECs starting from the Crown and moving down to the Root, neutralizing each one of the character BECs in the process.

Before you can begin Breathing through the Centres, it is important to establish a grounding cord for your body. Australian actress and director Kerry Dwyer (and then several years later, also Suzanne Ingleton) introduced me to the idea of a grounding cord in 1994 during rehearsals for *Hedda Gabler* by Henrik Ibsen.[7] The idea of a grounding cord is to establish a root connection with the earth before opening up the energetic Centres of the body. This not only assures you won't become disoriented, dizzy or a little 'spacey', but also engages the body energy system with that of the earth.

Grounding Cord Exercise

This exercise will connect your body energies to the centre of the earth.

- It is preferable to begin in a standing position, although some participants find it helpful to sit during the grounding cord and BEC breathing exercises in a chair or on the floor. This seated connection to the ground can also work very well.

- You may want to try both seated and standing positions to see which works best for you. With your eyes closed, feet shoulder-width apart, knees slightly bent and hips tucked in alignment with your spine.

---

[7] Directed by the author at the Ponton Theatre, Charles Sturt University, Bathurst, New South Wales 1994.

Figure 3.Grounding cord. Image from web[8]

1. Flex each foot, keeping your heel in touch with the floor and replace the foot back down on the ground, sensing all seven points of contact with the floor: five toes, outside of the foot and heel of the foot.

2. Make sure your knees are slightly bent throughout this exercise. Locked joints like knees, hips and ankles will block the energy flow.

3. Visualize a grounding cord that represents your breath energy moving through your body, down through the soles of your feet and into the floor.

4. Allow your grounding cord to move down through the floor, beneath the structure of the building and into the soil below.

---

[8] http://psychicsandiego.com/meditation_is_simple/html/partiii.htm.

Watch your grounding cord move through each layer of the earth, deeper and deeper until you reach the core of the earth.

5. Attach your grounding cord to the core. Allow it to find its own method of attachment Some actors engaged the following images:
    •   a grappling hook that hooks onto a bar in the centre of the earth;
    •   an intricate root system;
    •   a metal rod that melts into the molten core;
    •   an umbilical cord;
    •   a powerful light ray.

6. When you have connected your cord to the centre of the earth, travel back up through each layer of the earth until you reach the surface. This may happen very quickly or quite slowly; just allow your body to work at its own speed.

7. As you arrive at the surface, travel up into the heights of the earth's atmosphere, still connected to the core of the earth with your grounding cord. You will find your cord very flexible and elastic. Now find your way back along your grounding cord into this room, into this space, into your body, into your breath.

To ground or earth the body at the beginning of this work is paramount. Once we are earthed it becomes much easier to journey with expanded consciousness.

Part Two: Breathing Through the BEC's

Breathing through the Centres is a warm up exercise involving rapid breathing into each BEC from the Root to the Crown. The basis for this exercise was taught to me by Australian actor, director and author Suzanne Ingleton, who also works shamanically in her performances and teaching. The breathing technique uses rapid, short breaths in and out of the mouth as you focus on each BEC, one at a time, spending approximately two to three minutes on each one.

Recommended music for this Breathing exercise; OSHO Chakra Breathing Meditation

This rapid breathing into each one of the BECs energizes these Centres, allowing you to feel and understand the quality of energy in each Centre. As you process this information in each breathing session you will establish a library of information about each of your BECs that will inform your acting choices with the BECs further on. The breathing exercise will prepare your energetic body each day for the exercises that follow in this book.

Preparation

Air connects everything on this earth. It does not stop because it crosses country borders, enters into different religious ceremonies, bodies or governments. Air transports energy throughout our earthly system, we breathe it, move through it and sigh into it. It is a pathway to all aspects of life including our consciousness located in each of the Body Energy Centres.

With your eyes closed, relax your throat, jaw, facial muscles and breathe in and out of a slightly open mouth. Keep your jaw relaxed, your throat open and allow your breath to pass through your body, inhaling and exhaling. The rhythm for this breath is like the panting of a dog on a hot day.

Some actors find it easier to focus on the out breath, others on the in breath. Although it might seem as though your mouth will dry up or you might get dizzy, you will find that neither actually occurs. The body will balance itself as you breathe through each Centre; you can always swallow and reduce the amount of air you are breathing in and out. It might help you to imagine that the air you are breathing is like fuel to an engine and you are fueling your Body Energy Centres in order to work effectively with them.

Part of the magic of this breathing exercise is that you can regulate the intensity of the breath for varied experiences. You will find that some Centres feel closed, weak, open or difficult to connect with. This is an indication of the way you have been using or not using these Body Energy Centres and should provide invaluable feedback to you. For instance, if your body has a closed or blocked Belly Centre then it might be difficult for you to deeply connect with a character that has an open one, and playing a sexually active and passionately creative role may be challenging. To know that this Centre needs attention will give you vital information towards establishing the 'neutral body' that so many acting approaches strive for.

Grounded and relaxed, you are now ready to breathe through each of the Body Energy Centres. From a common breath rhythm (best helped with a CD or cassette of music designed for this breath work such as *Osho Chakra Breathing Meditation*) pick up the pace of your breathing together with the music and the ground until you are panting, continuing to allow the breath to flow in and out and keeping your jaw relaxed.

Breathing Rhythm and Color Imagery

The colors associated with each Centre are suggested with many different systems of chakra work. I have found it often helps an actor to focus on a color when first discovering the Body Energy Centre. For instance, red is a dense, more solid vibration, and the movement through to the lighter, more subtle violet color is not unlike an aspect of Grotowski's work in 1986 with his theory of Verticality. Described by Lisa Woolford as, "Verticality – we can see this phenomenon in categories of energy: heavy but organic energies (linked to the forces of life, to instincts, to sensuality) and other energies, more subtle. The question of verticality means to pass from a so-called coarse level – in a certain sense, an 'everyday level'- to a level of energy more subtle or even toward the higher connection".[9]

---

[9] Richards 1995: 125.

If visualizing the color suggested with each Body Energy Centre does not help you engage with that Centre, then simply focus on the Centre without the color. Often a color or image will come to you.

Root BEC:

Red – the shade of red is up to you. I tend to use a ruby red as it is soft, warm, deep and gentle. Let images of red objects, shapes and structures come to you such as roses, shirts, curtains etc., until you find one that suits you, then use it each time you work with this Centre.

Visualize a glowing spiral of energy based in your Root BEC, sending energy from this Centre down into the earth below. As you rapidly breathe in and out, visualize the spiral of energy coming from your Root Centre and moving down into the earth. Place your consciousness within that Centre as you breathe, stay present and relaxed as you allow the energy of that Centre to guide you.

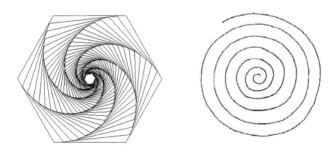

Figure 4. Images of energy patterns associated with the grounding cord

Belly BEC:

Orange – again, the shade is up to you. Some images I find helpful are: oranges; paintings of flowers; orange clothes.

Continuing the panting breath, breathe into this Centre just below the navel. You may find it helpful to sway or rock your hips to the beat of your breath, continuing to connect this energy Centre with the space around you. As you place your awareness into this Centre, relax the rest of your body and remember that the energy radiates in all directions from this Centre beyond the physical body. Place your awareness in this Centre and be receptive to what this Centre tells you.

Solar Plexus BEC:

Yellow – tune into the shade/image that works best for you: the sun; sunflowers; canaries; bananas; daffodils.

Your third BEC is your Solar, which is centered in the cradle of your rib cage. You may find it helpful to isolate your rib cage and articulate your spine to the beat of your breath, continuing to connect this Energy Centre with the space around you. Continuing the panting breath with the music, breathe through your Solar Plexus BEC, radiating your breath energy through this Centre and out into space around you on all sides. Visualize the glowing orb of yellow light seated in your Solar Plexus BEC, sending energy from this Centre out beyond your body and sending rays of light from your breath energy into the air around you, filling the room.

Heart BEC:

Green – I use an emerald shade of green, often imagining my whole chest is an emerald, radiating green light, out into the space around me: grass; chrysophrase; trees; clothes; countryside.

The fourth BEC is your Heart, which is centered in the middle of your chest. Again, continue the panting breath with the music, breathing through your Heart Centre, sending your breath energy through this Centre and out into the space around you on all sides. You may find it helpful to extend and sway your arms to the beat of your breath, continuing to connect this Energy Centre with the space around you. Visualize the glowing green light seated in your Heart BEC sending energy from this Centre and out beyond your body.

Throat BEC:

Blue – I often use a sky blue or powder blue rather than a dark blue, but again, see what comes to you: sky; water; eyes; cornflowers; irises; bluebirds; the sea.

The Throat BEC is centered in the middle of your neck. Continue the panting breath, breathing through your Throat BEC, sending your breath energy through this Centre into the room around you. Visualize the glowing orb of blue light seated in your Throat BEC, sending energy from this Centre out beyond your body, filling the room with radiation from this Body Energy Centre.

Mind BEC:

Indigo – this can be challenging. I follow the color blue into purple (in my mind's eye) and move back along the spectrum to the place where they both meet, where the edge of blue meets the edge of purple.

Your sixth BEC is centered in the middle of and behind your forehead. Continuing the panting breath with the music, breathe through your Mind BEC, send your breath energy through this Centre and out into space around you on all sides. You may find it helpful to move your head to the beat of your breath, continuing to connect this energy Centre with the space around you.

Visualize the glowing orb of indigo light seated in your Mind BEC sending energy from this Centre and out beyond your body, rays of light emerging from your breath energy and into the air around you, filling the room with radiation from this Body Energy Centre.

Crown BEC:

Violet – this can be a light shade like amethyst or deep like a violet: lavender; violets; royal robes. Your seventh BEC is your Crown, which is centered in the top of your head and extends up into the atmosphere. Continuing the panting breath with the music, breathe through your Crown BEC, sending breath energy through this Centre and up into the space above you, for as high as you like. You may find it helpful to raise and extend your arms to the beat of your breath, continuing to connect this Energy Centre with the space above you. Visualize the glowing orb of violet light seated in your Crown BEC sending energy from this Centre and out beyond your body, rays of light emerging from your breath energy and into the air above you, filling the room with radiation from this Body Energy Centre.

Breathing Back Down

Begin to gradually slow your breathing and spend time taking your breath energy back down through each BEC: Crown, Mind, Throat, Heart, Solar Plexus, Belly and Root. Once you have breathed through each Centre, relax your breathing back to normal, slowly roll your head onto your chest, then continue towards the floor as though touching your feet. Allow your arms and head to hang loosely and as you reach the floor, allowing your hands to connect with the floor. It is important to keep your knees bent. As your hands contact the floor, gently come down onto all fours, then stretch out and roll over onto your back. Listen to your body and notice where the energy is moving, how connected different parts of the body are and how you are feeling. Relax and notice your breath without trying to control it. Bring your self back into the room and when you are ready, open your eyes and reflect on today's session of BEC breathing. You may want to chart, illustrate or chronicle your experiences in a journal for reflection.

The fundamental component to the Body Energy Centre training is the BEC breathing, in which actors spend approximately 40 minutes of guided imagistic exploration as they breathe through their seven BECs. The BECs are closely related to the chakras in terms of their location and emotional content but are distinctly different in the sense that they serve a functional rather than overtly spiritual purpose (although the spiritual realm is certainly not closed in this system) and in the sense that McCutcheon has carefully adapted the language, philosophy and utility of the BECs specifically for the purpose of training performers.[10]

Part Three: Dancing Through the BEC's

This is an excellent warm up activity, as it loosens the muscles and joints and increases circulation of oxygen and blood throughout all of your Body Energy Centres.

You may want to experiment with *dancing* the BECs before *breathing* the BECs. Many actors have found that dancing both relaxes their daily tensions and also focuses their energies. They are able to travel more deeply into their experience with the breathing as a result.

Musical Accompaniment

It is important that you find musical accompaniment that resonates for you and your group. West African, African Caribbean and other diasporic musical forms offer very good accompaniment for this exercise. However, any instrumental music with a strong, continuous polyrhythm that is open-ended enough to allow you to discover your own energetic response is good for this.

Preparation

As with the breathing of the BECs, it is essential that you establish your grounding cord before beginning the dance. In preparation,

---

[10] Mary Elizabeth Anderson, from page 7 of her Masters thesis, 2007, University of California, Davis.

sense your grounding cord's connection to each Body Energy Centre and allow this sensation to resonate through each physical location and out into the energy beyond your body.

Once you have established your grounding cord, relax your shoulders and neck and, keeping a slight bend in your knees, align your hips so that they are in accordance with your body's spinal alignment. Take note of the relative tension and relaxation in each Body Energy Centre and its connected muscular-skeletal system.

Eyes gently closed, begin to move slowly in time with the music. This may take the form of rocking or swaying back and forth, shifting your weight from foot to foot. With these first movements, continue to survey your physical landscape and note how the musical and gravitational vibrations passing through are affecting each BEC and its corresponding muscles and bones.

Allow yourself to give into the desire to stretch any particularly tense regions and stretch your limbs with extended movement through space.

Once you have warmed up sufficiently and feel comfortable in your timing with the musical accompaniment, allow the dance to manifest itself in each of the Body Energy Centres. You may start with the Root and travel up to the Crown or you may dance between BECs, freely playing with each one to remind your body of the sensation in each Centre.

With the dance, allow the Body Energy Centre to *move* you. While breathing into and through each BEC, allow that breath energy to dance your entire body with the sensation of each area.

It is important to note the *different levels of consciousness* and awareness you experience when focusing on each BEC.

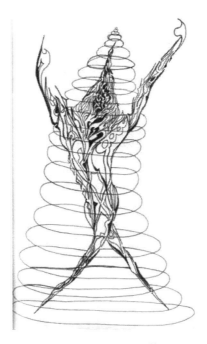

Figure 5. The Dance [11]

Here are some characteristics of the Body Energy Centres along with examples of how they often move participants in the dance:

Root
Recall that the Root BEC is related to your basic needs, your survival skills and your relationship to your body and the environment in terms of essential sustenance. While dancing the Root BEC, allow your energy to pass directly through your Root and into the floor, permitting this primal energy to move you back and forth as well as across the floor. Notice where this energy vibrates in the rest of your limbs: where do you feel tension? In your arms, your neck, your head? You will feel the strength of your thighs and calves as they ground you and direct your intent.

---

[11] Image by author 1984.

Belly

Bringing the dance into the Belly BEC, you will begin to feel the dexterity and fluidity of your hips and upper thighs. Allow your hips to swing, to sway, to rock forward, back and sideways, to change direction, swivel and spiral. Let the Belly BEC help you discover the potential in your hips and allow that movement and momentum to affect the rest of your torso, legs, arms and head. I often think of dances like the Hula from Hawaii with this BEC.

Solar

The Solar BEC connects us to our personal will and direction. This BEC helps us to accomplish difficult tasks, carry out plans, motivate and steer our future. Bring this direction and focus through your Solar BEC and allow it to push your body through the space at the musical tempo. How do these vibrations and movements connect to your limbs, your head, and the space around you? Let this energy travel in waves from the Solar BEC and out into the rest of your dancing body.

Heart

As the music travels into your Heart BEC, feel your chest cavity opening, connecting with the air and energy around your upper torso, and pulling you forward and back, side to side. Allow your arms to extend from the emerald green ball of energy, resonating in the centre of your chest and out into the rehearsal environment. Remember to focus the energy in a 360 degree radius all around your body, letting the energy from your Heart BEC move through your limbs. The Heart Centre is the seat of your compassionate, unconditional love. Allow this openness and generosity to pass through your Heart BEC and out into the rehearsal room. Let these sensations carry you to new locations in the room, discovering the architectural and interpersonal dynamics of today's rehearsal environment.

Throat

The Throat BEC is your vehicle for communicating and articulating your voice in the world — your literal voice with vocal cords and folds; your creative voice; your unique perspective with and connection to the world. As this Centre opens, feel the cavity in the middle of your neck, between your vocal cords and spine, expand

and fill with light beams that shoot out in every direction for 360 degrees. You are radiating from your collar bone to the point at which your head meets your neck. Allow your neck and head to respond to the rhythm of the music, gently rotating from side to side, back and forth.

Mind
The Mind BEC is the seat of your analytical and critical capacities. This BEC engages our ability to reflect, interpret and theorize. Feel your cranial cavity – between your temples, between your forehead and scalp – open and expand in response to the immense capacity of your thought power, your philosophical perspective, and your membership as part of a collective unconscious. Where does this energy take you around the room? Leading from the Mind Centre, where do these energetic vibrations travel in the rest of your body? You may want to massage your temples and touch the base of your skull and back of your hairline to remind yourself of the capacity of this Centre. There are several possibilities with this BEC depending on whether you focus the energy into the centre or going out into the room from the centre.

Crown
Finding your way to the Crown, you are finding your connection between your body and the universe. While the Root BEC grounded you and connected you on a survival level to your environment, the Crown BEC reminds you of your spiritual self, your metaphysical self. You should begin to feel the energy rise up through the top of your scalp and into the ethers above you. You may want to touch the top of your head while allowing the spiral of energy to rotate your head and neck. Being mindful of your spinal alignment, continue to feel the energy of the Crown BEC lift your body from its Root and into the cosmos.

By breathing and dancing through the BECs you will develop an ability to focus your attention, breath, voice and movement through any one or combination of the BECs. When you feel you have some control and understanding of your BECs, dance with different combinations of BECs and notice the affect this has on your posture, voice and feelings. For example, try dancing with just your Root and

Heart open, then add a closed Belly, you will soon see the possibilities are endless for creating characters through this method.

Part Four: Exploring the BEC's

What follows in this section is a series of exercises that prepare your body for working with the BECs in character preparation and development and scene work.

Exercise One

Walk around the space, relaxing your body as you walk, notice the way your feet are making contact with the floor and the way your ankle moves as you place your foot on the floor. Continue walking, noticing the way your foot, ankle and knee work together and then follow this movement through to the hip and into the body torso, through the spine, rib cage, shoulders, neck and head. Continue walking until you feel connected from foot to head.

Walking through the BECs.

Take time to notice each Centre and what happens to the rest of your body when you place your focus on different BECs.

1. Start with the ROOT, breathing into that area as you walk, allowing the energy to flow from the Centre of the Root BEC through your legs, down into the ground and deep into the earth. Allow the energy to return up the legs into the Root and then feel the difference of energy leaving the Root, back into the earth, and energy coming up from the earth into the Root. Try not to have any focus of energy above the Root — so your hips, belly, chest, shoulders, arms, hands and head will have no 'vital' or active energy moving through them. You may feel a little like an ape or a very basic kind of person, which is good. The movement associated with the Root is very much a downward movement into the earth. As

mentioned earlier, it helps to think of the many indigenous dances you may have seen from American Indian, African and Aboriginal dancers and to notice that much of their dancing energy involves a kind of 'stomping' into the ground, as though they are driving energy through their legs into the earth. This kind of dancing helps to wake up the Root BEC.

2. Move your focus to the BELLY, the area approximately one to two inches below your navel. Try to place your awareness, as you breathe, right in the centre of the Belly BEC, as though you had drawn a line from the surface of your skin below the navel to the centre of your body between the belly skin and the spine.

3. Once you have determined the centre of this BEC you can then expand its size in a circular manner until the energy of this Centre extends out past your physical body. Play with bringing the size of the BEC to the size of a grapefruit then to the size of a large light ball. This might be large enough to fill the room or large enough to extend from your Belly BEC to a foot beyond your skin. Allow your body to respond to the attention and breath you give this BEC. Let your body fall around it and see what happens as the Belly BEC becomes the place from which every impulse originates.

4. Walk around the space focusing on the Solar Plexus BEC, the Heart BEC and the Mind BEC. Start with all three open and experience how your posture and walk is affected.

5. Now close the Heart and Solar Plexus BECs and feel what that does to your walk, your breathing, and your attitude.

6. Keep the Mind BEC open and add the Solar Plexus BEC, by 'add' I mean open this BEC also. Notice again your posture, walk, breathing and attitude.

7. Now add the Heart BEC so that you have all three Centres open again. Be aware of the relationship between each

Centre as you open and close them, noticing that a particular state of 'awareness' or 'consciousness' comes with each BEC. It is different in the closed state compared with the open state and will be different also in a leaking state.

Part Five: Open, Closed, leaking BEC's

Identifying whether a Centre is open or closed relies a great deal on what you experience when you breathe and move through these Centres in the previous exercises. If you have trouble feeling a Centre after several days of work, then it is safe to assume that this Centre is closed or functioning at a greatly reduced level.

Try closing a Centre you feel is open and accessible and see what that feels like. Then open it again and note how different it feels. Then try going back to the closed Centre, breathe into it and stay focused until you feel some energy moving within.

As Centres open that have been closed for a while, you will find that the newly released energies will affect your body, mind and emotions in different ways. In fact, if you consider 'e-motion' to be *energy in motion* you will find the release of old energy as 'e-motion' a rewarding result of the work. For a Centre to be free and open it needs to be free of the old energies that kept it closed. The true 'neutral body' is an open one, able to express from all Centres. Once the Body Energy Centres are open, it becomes easier to play around with opening and closing them.

There are three major BEC states:

1. OPEN
2. CLOSED
3. LEAKING

1. OPEN

Choose one of the Body Energy Centres to work with.

1. As you walk around the space, breathe into this BEC, imagining a kind of 'central headquarters' right in the centre of your body in relation to the position of this BEC. For example, as you think about the Solar BEC, move inwards to the point that is halfway between the skin on your back and the skin on your front.

2. Once you have located the centre of the BEC, imagine a circle of energy radiating out from it on all sides. Breathe this circle into larger and larger sizes until you are meeting the walls of the space you are working in.

3. Then, using your breath, bring the size of the circle back in until it is surrounding the very centre of this BEC. These circles might also be seen as' rings' of energy.

4. Stand in one space with feet hip width apart, knees slightly bent and quietly speak a line of text from this BEC. Imagine the BEC itself is talking and allow the rest of your body to fall around this impulse. In other words, do not consciously try to move any muscles that are not being moved by the BEC as it tries to speak.

5. Explore the voice by using your breath and placing your awareness along different rings of energy that are coming from this BEC. Some of the rings might be large and fill the room. Some might be small and intimate, hardly breaking through the skin.

6. Next, start to walk around the space as you speak the line of text from this BEC. Notice how your body wants to move in order to accommodate your full focus on this one Centre. Your posture, breathing, walk and gestures will all be greatly influenced.

This is a useful exercise to do with each BEC depending on the ease or difficulty with which you can do it; you will know whether this Centre is one that has been closed for some time. The following is an observation made by an actor as he worked with opening the Heart BEC.

> I remember very early in the rehearsal process on a particular BEC breathing experience where my heart became more open. Simply concentrating on opening this area brought about a specific emotional response helping me prepare for my work of the day. My own inhibitions were released, thus freeing my acting. Later, when I rehearsed the role of Caldwell B. Cladwell in the musical *Urinetown*, I continued to experiment with the BECs. I found that using a strong root and a closed heart helped me in scenes when I needed to dominate. I would then open my heart whenever my daughter was in the room, except when I finally betray her.[12]

2. CLOSED

Begin with standing in one spot, legs hip width apart, knees slightly bent and choose one BEC to work with. Notice your breathing and how it changes as you close that BEC.

Think of the many different ways you might close these Centres. Images of closing doors, metal doors clanking shut, roll-a-door coming down, boarding up the entrance or pulling down a powerful blind might come to mind.

1. Try speaking a line of text through this closed BEC and notice what happens to the voice. Where is it placed if the BEC is closed?

2. Now try opening that BEC and speaking the line of text. There should be a noticeable difference.

---

[12] MFA Actor, Jesse Merz, Department of Theatre and Dance, University of California, Davis.

3. Walk around the room using your breath to close the BEC once again, allowing the body to fall around it without judging. As you deliver the line of text again notice what your body has to do in order to accommodate this closed Centre.
4. How does it change your posture? Your voice? Your gestures? Your attitude?

When a Centre is closed there is no energy coming from that part of the body, which automatically forces energies to work through other Centres in a different way. This becomes interesting as you observe your body energy and tune into where it is moving and through which Centre it most wants to express itself.

When you look at the following image you might see that the actor is very focused in his Mind BEC. The jaw is thrust forward in a way that disconnects the throat energy from the head. Relaxing his mind and placing the idea of a 'mind' or a place of consciousness into the Throat BEC and breathing through that should open up the throat and relax the jaw.

Figure 6. Author with Daniel [13] working with closed throat BEC. Photo by Brooke Wagstaff.

---

[13] Daniel Giles, Theatre major, Department of Theatre and Dance, University of California, Davis. 2004.

3. LEAKING

If you imagine an exhausted mother who has a collapsed Solar Plexus Centre and an over-used Heart Centre, you will see a 'leaking' Centre. The Heart Centre has been the main mode of expression for this person, to the detriment of the other Centres. All her body energy has been pouring out of this Centre as she gives and gives until finally it just leaks constantly. Apply this to each of the BECs and you will see what these leaking or exhausted Centres do to posture, voice and gesture.

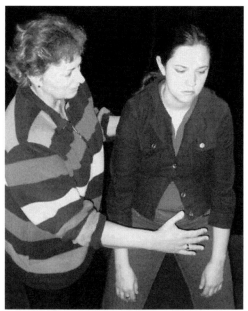

Figure 7. Author and MFA actor Katie Rubin
exploring Leaking Heart Centre and collapsed
Solar Centre. Photo by Brooke Wagstaff.

Looking at the above image you can see that the middle of the body is collapsed into itself as the leaking Heart overwhelms the other BECs' ability to function. Breathing deeply into the Solar BEC will automatically open up and strengthen the middle of the body, while taking strain off the back and shoulders. By placing your hands over the Heart BEC and breathing your energy back into the body through this BEC, you will start to return it to a more neutral position.

The key aspect of a leaking BEC is that it has been over-used as a component of the personality 'face' and is, therefore, tired and exhausted. The level of energy coming from a leaking BEC will be as low as a dripping tap: it is a Centre that has lost its vital force.

Often the effect of this leaking BEC on the body is one that will pull the posture out of alignment. For instance, a leaking Heart BEC will often thrust the top section of the ribcage associated with this BEC forward, this then pushes the shoulders and neck back resulting in a kind of 'slumping'. This will in turn affect the way the body breathes and the nature of the voice as it attempts to move through that Centre.

1. While walking around the room, select one BEC you'd like to work with, first close it up and notice what restrictions this gives to that area.
2. Now, release that BEC by opening it, allowing energy to rush out of that Centre into the room. It is a good idea to work with your breath, using inhalation and exhalation in rhythm with opening and closing the BEC.
3. Continue to release energy and breath through this Centre until you feel as though your body is 'slumping' around the BEC, resulting in a feeling of collapse or draining around the Centre you are working with.
4. What happens when you push this BEC into a place of leaking? Allow your body to look and feel out of shape, your breathing to change, your walk and your posture to change.
5. Return back to neutral by breathing into this BEC and drawing the energy back into it. Try a quick 'systems check' on all the BECs to make sure they are as much in balance as possible.
6. Keep moving around the room breathing several times into each BEC.[14]

---

[14] For more detailed feedback from actors who have been working with this approach, see Appendix 1.

Focus Your Attention

As with most actor training exercises, the greatest benefit comes from the use of breath and focus. Nurturing your power of intention and attention will also bring fruitful results. There is no absolute right or wrong when working with the Body Energy Centres. The key is to trust what you experience, to be aware and to make these exercises a daily practice. Your body will soon teach you about your BECs and provide you with images, colors and states of consciousness that are unique to your body and who you are.

CHAPTER THREE

Using BECs to Create Your Character

In his book *Creating A Role*, Stanislavsky writes; "Let me repeat that the best thing that can happen to an actor is to have his whole role form itself in him of its own accord. In such instances, one can forget about all 'systems', techniques, and give oneself up wholly to the power of magic nature".[1] He also points out to his actors that "this alas, did not happen to any of you,"[2] suggesting why there is a need for systems and methods. Sometimes an actor is lucky enough for the role to form itself, but usually we all need a variety of exercises and approaches to assist us in developing the role or character. Potentially all these exercises are journeys carefully planned to enhance the actor's process of creation.

This chapter is a journey into character. It will address the integration of BECs into the creation of character and the delivery of text. This work is not intended to replace the necessary work of text analysis, unit breakdown, identifying of beats and actions, but to be used as an additional step towards deepening the journey the actor takes in creating a character.[3]

> The key is to simply give over to the process.
> Again, you are not being asked to change your

---

[1] Stanislavsky 1965: 151.
[2] Ibid.
[3] Thankfully, Stanislavsky has set down a wonderful guide for the actor in preparation to play a character in *An Actor Prepares* and *Creating A Role*, I would urge every actor to read this book.

religion or to check your common sense at the
door. Instead, just throw yourself into the work.
Close your eyes and allow images of the energy
of the centres to envelope you. Simply imagine
the exercise as an adventure in clarity and
physical articulation. Soon you'll notice that you
have a grander range of motion in specific areas. [4]

Figure 8. Jesse Merz (left) and Matt Moore in *Myth, Propaganda and Disaster in Nazi Germany and Contemporary America*.[5]

The journey a character takes through a play often requires that a change occurs in one way or another: maybe learning takes place or a new awareness is found. Transformation of the self into a believable character requires a shift in consciousness which will allow the presence of another character/personality to exist as an expanded part of 'self.' Focusing on a particular Centre for this change can create a real transformation of energy. Referring to Chapter Two and the descriptions of these three BEC states might be useful here.

---

[4] Jesse Merz, MFA actor, Department of Theatre and Dance, University of California, Davis.
[5] By Stephen Sewell, performed at Mondavi Center for the Performing Arts, University of California, Davis. October 2006.

The following section is from an actor's journal, referring to a scene she scored using the BECs in Australian playwright Stephen Sewell's *Myth, Propaganda and Disaster in Nazi Germany and Contemporary America*, which I directed in 2006 at the Studio Theatre, Mondavi Centre for the Performing Arts, University of California, Davis. She was working solely with the open state of the BECs at this time. "Several weeks into the rehearsal process, I returned to my script and actually charted out various versions of the scenes using the Body Energy Centres as part of my strategies and tactics. While my actual onstage choices varied considerably by the time we got to performance, I found it necessary to actually script some initial "plays" in order to track the dynamic between Eve and other characters in her world in real time as opposed to her imagined time. For example, see the scene below as I charted it:

Therapist: Is that why you feel so angry? **Mind BEC (intent: control and direct)**
Eve: Angry? Do you think I feel angry? **Heart BEC (intent: passively receive)**
Therapist: You sound angry. **Mind BEC (intent: do not let her evade question)**
Eve: Do I? **Heart BEC (intent: destabilize interrogation by softening)**
Therapist: Do you think it's my fault? **Mind BEC (intent: make her uncomfortable)**
Eve: No. **Crown BEC (intent: escape unreasonable situation)**
Therapist: Do you think it's your husband's? **Mind BEC (intent: keep on course)**
Eve: Do I sound angry? **Crown BEC (intent: continue to escape further away)**
Therapist: Yes. **Mind BEC (intent: wrangle her back into conversation).** [6]

---

[6] Mary Elizabeth Anderson, MFA and Ph. D student, Department of Theatre and Dance, University of California, Davis.

Figure 9. Mary Elizabeth Anderson as Eve (left) and Ashanti Newton as the
Therapist in *Myth, Propaganda and Disaster in Nazi Germany and
Contemporary America.*[7]

In this case, it helped the actor to add the qualities of that BEC, as
well as the intent behind the text. It added another layer of energies
she was emitting towards the other actor without detracting from the
intention of the text. In an unexpected way, the actor moved from
exploration with the BECs to a beat analysis.

> Regardless of the style of text you are working
> with, the BECs will give you access to particular
> energy Centres in the body just as a flute player
> has access to every note. Using the BECs
> broadens the spectrum of choices you can make in
> any given moment of the play. BECs are internal
> so it's easier to access my own internal feelings
> and energies – with other processes it (the
> technique) is applied rather than accessed.[8]

---

[7] By Stephen Sewell, performed at Mondavi Center for the Performing Arts,
University of California, Davis. October 2006.
[8] Tom McCauley, MFA actor, Department of Theatre and Dance at University of
California, Davis.

Figure 10. Tom McCauley as Willy Loman, University of California, Davis 2006.

Following are some exercises for developing your ability to use the BECs in the creation of a character.

Exercise One: Tuning into the BECs

It is important to start with a body as free of stress as possible. One way to achieve this is to do the BEC breathing exercise explained in Chapter Two. If you have already done this today then the following exercise is easy and relatively quick. Bring your body back to neutral by just walking and breathing through each of the BECs.

- As you walk around the room, empty your mind of all chatter and focus just on the breath, watching and feeling it move through your nose, into your Root BEC and out of your mouth.
- Take at least five breaths into the Root before you move to the Belly, the Solar, the Heart, the Throat, the Mind and finally, the Crown. Observe how your awareness changes, as

each BEC becomes connected not only through the breath but also *with* the breath.

- After you reach the Crown, bring your awareness and breathe down to the Mind, giving two to three breaths to each BEC, working your way down to the Root.
- When you are at the Root, come to a standstill, feet shoulder width apart, knees bent, flop over to touch your toes and exhale at the same time. Stay in this position for three deep breaths, allowing the arms, head, neck and shoulders to relax as your spine stretches.
- Return to a relaxed standing position and choose a BEC to work with.
- Ask this BEC to walk your body around the room; relax, breathe into the BEC and hand over control to it.
- Observe how your body responds to the impulses of this Centre.
- Choose another BEC and repeat the exercise, noticing how differently your body responds to this BEC compared with the first one.
- Continue choosing BECs, asking them to walk your body around the room, trying to suspend all judgments, allowing your body to respond in ways you had never imagined.

What you are doing, by allowing the BEC to walk the body, is engaging with the 'mind' or *consciousness* of that particular part of the body energy. I have found it useful to tune in to my state of awareness when I am thinking, knowing my intent is focused in my mind I can focus on how that affects my body, if every movement I make comes only from that Centre. This gives me a good idea of how one Centre that I am familiar with feels. Then to explore the other Centres I take that image my mind and place it into each Centre as though I am actually 'thinking' from that Centre.

I've also found it helpful to imagine my mouth or eyes or ears in each Centre, to breathe from the back or sides into each Centre and to generally place my known systems of awareness, the five senses, into each Centre.

To start, focus only on the Mind BEC.

1. OPENING

Open and breathe through this Centre, remembering it is not just accessible from the front of the body but also the sides and the back.

- One of the images I love for this Centre is a saucer-like spaceship with many small windows around its edge. A small blue alien being moves around inside the spaceship (my mind) and opens each of the windows, one at a time, letting in light with each opening, until the centre of the ship is illuminated from all sides.
- Choose some text to work with and speak some lines of text through this Centre as you place your full awareness into this Centre. Imagine your mouth in the middle of your Mind BEC and allow your voice to move through this Centre. Try to allow this Centre to do the speaking and communicating.
- If you are not sure whether you're speaking through your Mind BEC, bring the voice back to your throat and mouth and note if there's a difference; then send the voice through the Mind BEC again.

2. CLOSING

Now close the Mind BEC and speak the same lines again, be aware of how you use the breath when the Centre is closed.

- One of the best ways to get a clear sense of what a closed Centre feels like is to open it, speak the text, then close it and speak the text. Continue doing this until you have a full sense of the difference.
- Observe what it does to your posture, your awareness and your tone and quality of voice.
- An image I often use for a closed Centre is boards across a door.

3. LEAKING

Open the Mind BEC and leak the energy out of it, a little like a
dripping tap that you cannot control.

- Experiment with varying degrees of 'leakage', from a drip to
  a river with little or no energy.
- Use the text with each state of leaking and decide for
  yourself which works best.

Exercise Two: Working with the Three BEC States

Repeat Exercise One using two BECs instead of one, for example the
Belly BEC and the Heart BEC. This allows for nine different
combinations which are shown in the table below using the following

Legend

Closed	*	
Open	o	
Leaking	>	

Table 1

	BELLY	**HEART**
1	o Open	* Closed
2	o Open	> Leaking
3	o Open	o Open
4	* Closed	o Open
5	* Closed	> Leaking
6	* Closed	* Closed
7	> Leaking	o Open
8	> Leaking	* Closed
9	> Leaking	> Leaking

For example, try working in detail with the following section of text
by Benedick from Act Two, Scene Three, *Much Ado About Nothing*
by William Shakespeare.

Benedick:

This can be no trick: the conference was sadly borne.
They have the truth of this from Hero.
They seem to pity the lady:
It seems her affections have their full bent.
Love me! Why, it must be requited.
I hear how I am censured:
they say I will bear myself proudly,
if I perceive the love come from her;
they say too that she will rather die than give any sign of
affection.
I did never think to marry: I must not seem proud:
Happy are they that hear their detractions and can put
them to mending. They say the lady is fair – 'tis a
truth, I can bear them witness: and virtuous – 'tis
so, I cannot reprove it: and wise, but for loving
me – by my troth, it is no addition to her wit, nor
no great argument of her folly, for I will be
horribly in love with her. I may chance have some
odd quirks and remnants of wit broken on me,
because I have railed so long against marriage: but
doth not the appetite alter?
a man loves the meat in his youth that he cannot endure in
his age.
Shall quips and sentences and these paper bullets of
the brain awe a man from the career of his humour?
No – the world must be peopled. When I said I would
die a bachelor, I did not think I should live till I
were married. [9]

Take one line and break it up into phrases. Assign two BECs to each phrase and work with these repeatedly for one to two hours at a time. You will be training each BEC through repetition just as a piano player trains her hands by playing scales. Try not to expect any particular results for the first few sessions, but allow your body to

---

[9] *Much Ado About Nothing, The Complete Works of William Shakespeare.* 1988 : 133.

respond differently each time. You will find that each Centre will soon 'record' itself into your body response system and you will then enjoy experimenting with the three different states of Open, Leaking and Closed.

Repetition is one of the best ways to introduce a new concept to the body; even taking the first phrase "This can be no trick" and replaying it through every possible variation of BECs could take weeks or more until you feel you have any skill in the use of BECs.

Table 2

Character: **Benedick**	BEC	BEC
This can be no trick.	Belly o	Heart *
The conference was sadly borne	Belly >	Heart *
they have the truth of this from Hero	Belly o	Heart >
they seem to pity the lady	Belly *	Heart *
It seems her affections have their full bent.	Belly >	Heart >
Love me?	Belly o	Heart o

It is important to begin with small sections of text as you learn another way to work and listen with your body. You need to give your body time to fine tune its senses to the idea of the BECs changing and adapting at this pace. Once you have mastered these smaller sections of text, your body will respond more readily to the larger ones and your scoring might look a little like this:

Table 3

Character: **Benedick**	BEC	BEC
This can be no trick. The conference was sadly borne; they have the truth of this from Hero; they seem to pity the lady.	Belly o	Heart *
It seems her affections have their full bent. Love me? Why, it must be requited. I hear how I am censured	Belly *	Heart *
they have the truth of this from Hero	Belly o	Heart >
They say I will bear myself proudly if I perceive the love come from her. They say too that she will rather die than give any sign of affection.	Belly *	Heart *
I did never think to marry. I must not seem proud	Belly >	Heart >
Happy are they that hear their detractions and can put them to mending. They say the lady is fair – 'tis a truth, I can bear them witness; and virtuous – 'tis so,	Belly o	Heart o

Eventually, you will find yourself making choices naturally from the BECs without necessarily scoring every section. I believe it is important to keep the Body Energy Centres free and ready to use in a different way with each night's performance, since we know the dynamics change in every performance every night.

Remember this work is not replacing the text analysis and therefore should not alter the underlying meaning and intention of the text.

The character Phebe from *As You Like It* by William Shakespeare

Act Three, Scene Five

PHEBE:

Think not I love him, though I ask for him;
'Tis but a peevish boy – yet he talks well.
But what care I for words? Yet words do well
When he that speaks them pleases those that hear.
It is a pretty youth; not very pretty;
But sure he's proud; and yet his pride becomes him.
He'll make a proper man. The best thing in him
Is his complexion; and faster than his tongue
Did make offense, his eye did heal it up.
He is not very tall; yet for his year's he's tall.
His leg is but so so; and yet 'tis well.
There was a pretty redness in his lip,
A little riper and more lusty red
Than that mixed in his cheek; 'twas just the difference
Betwixt the constant red and mingled damask.
There be some women, Silvius, had they marked him
In parcels as I did, would have gone near
To fall in love with him; but, for my part,
I love him not nor hate him not; and yet
I have more cause to hate him than to love him;
For what had he to do to chide at me?
He said mine eyes were black and my hair black;
And, now I am rememb'red, scorned at me.
I marvel why I answered not again.
But that's all one; omittance is no quittance.
I'll write to him a very taunting letter,
And thou shalt bear it – wilt thou, Silvius?[10]

---

[10] *As You Like It, The Complete Works of William Shakespeare*, 1988: 125.

Table 4

Character: **Phebe**	BEC	BEC
Think not I love him, though I ask for him; 'Tis but a peevish boy; yet he talks well.	Belly o	Heart *
But what care I for words?	Belly *	Heart *
Yet words do well. When he that speaks them pleases those that hear.	Belly o	Heart >
It is a pretty youth; not very pretty; But sure he's proud; and yet his pride becomes him.	Belly >	Heart *
He'll make a proper man. The best thing in him Is his complexion;	Belly >	Heart >

Once you have the idea of moving from BEC to BEC and using the three states, you can try some variations.

Character: **Phebe**	BECs
Think not I love him, though I ask for him;	Belly o
'Tis but a peevish boy; yet he talks well.	Solar >
But what care I for words?	Throat *
It seems her affections have their full bent. Love me? Why, it must be requited. I hear how I am censured	Mind o
	Crown >
	Heart >
they have the truth of this from Hero	Solar o Heart *

They say I will bear myself proudly if I perceive the   Crown o
love come from her. They say too that she will   Solar o
rather die than give any sign of affection.
I did never think to marry. I must not seem proud   Mind * Heart *
Happy are they that hear their detractions and can   Throat o
put them to mending. They say the lady is fair – 'tis   Mind o
a truth, I can bear them witness; and virtuous – 'tis
so,

The use of these Centres is both simple and complex depending on how much and how often you want to work with them. It is possible to change BECs for every line of dialogue, much like a dancer in contact improvisation. Paula Dawson writes on her work with BECs; "BECs do not have an end, if I'm working with the idea of opposition there's only so far I can go but if using a BEC it continues and fills the room with all levels of consciousness and you may close it off but that energy is still out there. I can touch the back of the theatre with this energy. I used a lot of mapping of BECs, mapping becomes organic".[11]

Figure 11 Paula Dawson as Max in *Myth, Propaganda and Disaster in Nazi Germany and Contemporary America.*[12]

---

[11] Paula Dawson, MFA actor, Department of Theatre and Dance, University of California, Davis.
[12] By Stephen Sewell, performed at Mondavi Performing Arts Centre, University of California, Davis. October 2006.

The following are a few examples of a more complex range of choices once you've become familiar with using just one or two BECs as the key Centre for the character.

Exercise Three: Using the BEC states with *Hedda Gabler* by Henrik Ibsen

Looking at the character of Hedda in the play *Hedda Gabler* by Henrik Ibsen, we will explore some of the possible configurations of BECs. I chose this play because it was the first play in which I used the BEC and Shamanic Journey approaches with Theatre Media students at Charles Sturt University, Bathurst, New South Wales. To begin with, choose two BECs you can work with over the following short scenes which have been broken down into units based on characters entering or leaving the scene. For example, the opening scene with Miss Tesman and Berta is unit one; as Tesman enters unit two begins; when Berta leaves unit three begins; and Hedda entering is the start of unit four. The following exercise begins with unit four as the focus is on the main character of Hedda who enters in this unit.

Within each unit lies the usual potential for determining objectives, beats and motivations for the character, which hopefully will inform your final BEC choices for each unit. Ideally this approach should work hand in hand with more traditional approaches to text analysis and the playing of 'action.'

Please note that the following sections of text are segments and not the entire text of each unit.

Hedda Gabler. Act One: Unit Four. [13]

HEDDA *enters from the left through the inner room. Her face and figure show refinement and distinction. Her complexion is pale and opaque. Her steel-grey eyes express a cold, unruffled repose. Her*

---

[13] Text from Henrik Ibsen *Hedda Gabler*. Translation: Edmund Gosse and William Archer from The Project Gutenberg Etext. http://gutenberg.net.

hair is of an agreeable brown, but not particularly abundant. She is dressed in a tasteful, somewhat loose-fitting morning gown.

MISS TESMAN

[*Going to meet HEDDA*] Good morning, my dear Hedda! Good morning and a hearty welcome!

HEDDA

[*Holds out her hand.*] Good morning, dear Miss Tesman! So early a call! That is kind of you.

MISS TESMAN

[*With some embarrassment.*] Well, has the bride slept well in her new home?

HEDDA

Oh yes, thanks. Passably.

TESMAN

[*Laughing.*] Passably! Come, that's good, Hedda! You were sleeping like a stone when I got up.

HEDDA

Fortunately. Of course one has always to accustom one's self to new surroundings, Miss Tesman, little by little. [*Looking towards the left.*] Oh, there the servant has gone and opened the veranda door, and let in a whole flood of sunshine.

1. Try this scene using just three open BECs, Root, Mind and Solar. Run the unit a few times until you feel comfortable.

2. Now try running the unit using three closed BECS, Belly, Heart and Crown. What does that feel like? In your torso? Your arms? Your head? Your legs and feet?

3. Working with only the Leaking Throat BEC, run the unit again.

4. Now try putting them all together. This will take some practice, but you will see how having a clear focus with each BEC will result in a particular posture, vocal quality, attitude and character traits.

Below is an example of how you might chart this first unit using BECs.

Table 5

BEC	Unit 4	5	6	7
Crown	*			
Mind	o			
Throat	>			
Heart	*			
Solar	o			
Belly	*			
Root	*			

You will find that by practicing these exercises, your body, posture and voice will be determined by these Centres. As each Centre opens, closes or leaks, you will experience a different quality of voice, a changed posture and your body will experience another level of awareness and consciousness.

Once you feel you have this unit under control you can try playing around with other variations such as:

- Belly BEC open, Mind BEC closed. Notice what this does to your voice, posture and interactions with the other characters.

- Work this scene again with the Mind BEC leaking and the Belly BEC closed. Notice how this influences your character and the way you interact with the other characters.

Exercise Four: Continuing BEC work on Hedda Gabler

Unit Five begins just after Aunt Julia leaves in Act One. One possible BEC scenario for this unit is to simply change the *leaking* Throat to open and the Solar to *closed*.

Table 6

BEC	Unit 4	5	6	7
Pages				
Crown	*	*		
Mind	o	o		
Throat	>	o		
Heart	*	*		
Solar	o	*		
Belly	*	*		
Root	*	o		

[*In the meantime, HEDDA walks about the room, raising her arms and clenching her hands as if in desperation. Then she flings back the curtains from the glass door, and stands there looking out. Presently, TESMAN returns and closes the door behind him.*]

TESMAN

[*Picks up the slippers from the floor.*] What are you looking at, Hedda?

HEDDA

[*Once more calm and mistress of herself.*] I am only looking at the leaves. They are so yellow- so withered.

TESMAN

[*Wraps up the slippers and lays them on the table.*] Well, you see, we are well into September now.

HEDDA

[*Again restless.*] Yes, to think of it! Already in, in September.

TESMAN

Don't you think Aunt Julia's manner was strange, dear? Almost solemn? Can you imagine what was the matter with her? Eh?

HEDDA

I scarcely know her, you see. Is she not often like that?

TESMAN

No, not as she was to-day.

HEDDA

[*Leaving the glass door.*] Do you think she was annoyed about the bonnet?

TESMAN

Oh, scarcely at all. Perhaps a little, just at the moment…

HEDDA

But what an idea, to pitch her bonnet about in the drawing-room! No one does that sort of thing.

Unit Six. (The arrival of Mrs. Elvsted,)

What would happen if the Crown leaked and the Throat was closed, keeping the other BECs the same as Unit Five?

Table 7

BEC	Unit 4	5	6	7
Pages				
Crown	*	*	>	
Mind	o	o	o	
Throat	>	o	*	
Heart	*	*	*	
Solar	o	*	*	
Belly	*	*	*	
Root	*	o	o	

BERTA opens the door for MRS. ELVSTED and goes out herself. MRS. ELVSTED is a woman of fragile figure, with pretty, soft features. Her eyes are light blue, large, round, and somewhat prominent, with a startled, inquiring expression. Her hair is remarkably light, almost flaxen, and unusually abundant and wavy.

She is a couple of years younger than HEDDA. She wears a dark visiting dress, tasteful, but not quite in the latest fashion.

HEDDA

[*Receives her warmly.*] How do you do, my dear Mrs. Elvsted? It's delightful to see you again.

MRS. ELVSTED

[*Nervously, struggling for self-control.*] Yes, it's a very long time since we met.

TESMAN

[*Gives her his hand.*] And we too eh?

HEDDA

Thanks for your lovely flowers.

MRS. ELVSTED

Oh, not at all, I would have come straight here yesterday afternoon; but I heard that you were away.

TESMAN

Have you just come to town? Eh?

MRS. ELVSTED

I arrived yesterday, about midday. Oh, I was quite in despair when I heard that you were not at home.

HEDDA

In despair! How so?

TESMAN

Why, my dear Mrs. Rysing – I mean Mrs. Elvsted

HEDDA

I hope that you are not in any trouble?

MRS. ELVSTED

Yes, I am. And I don't know another living creature here that I can turn to.

HEDDA

[*Laying the bouquet on the table.*] Come, let us sit here on the sofa

MRS. ELVSTED

Oh, I am too restless to sit down.

HEDDA

Oh no, you're not. Come here. [*She draws MRS. ELVSTED down upon the sofa and sits at her side.*]

TESMAN

Well? What is it, Mrs. Elvsted ?

HEDDA

Has anything particular happened to you at home?

MRS. ELVSTED

Yes and no. Oh, I am so anxious you should not misunderstand me.

HEDDA

Then your best plan is to tell us the whole story, Mrs. Elvsted.

TESMAN

I suppose that's what you have come for eh?

MRS. ELVSTED

Yes, yes, of course it is. Well then, I must tell you, if you don't already know, that Eilert Lovborg is in town, too.

HEDDA

Lovborg !

TESMAN

What! Has Eilert Lovborg come back? Fancy that, Hedda!

HEDDA

Well well...I hear it.

Unit Seven, (The arrival of Judge Brack)

Table 8

BEC	Unit 4	5	6	7
Crown	*	*	>	*
Mind	o	o	o	o
Throat	>	o	*	o
Heart	*	*	*	*
Solar	o	*	*	o
Belly	*	*	*	o
Root	*	*	*	*

You will see that by opening up the Belly, Solar, Throat and Mind, Hedda has become more 'present' than in the previous units. She is particularly more open in her communication and creative energies, allowing her to spar and have some fun with Brack.

BERTA
[*Taking the letter.*] Yes, ma'am.

She opens the door for JUDGE BRACK and goes out herself.

JUDGE BRACK
[*With his hat in his hand, bowing.*] May one venture to call so early in the day?

HEDDA
Of course one may.

TESMAN
[*Presses his hand.*] You are welcome at any time. [*Introducing him.*] Judge Brack, Miss Rysing.

HEDDA
Oh!

BRACK
[*Bowing.*] Ah, delighted !

HEDDA
[*Looks at him and laughs.*] It's nice to have a look at you by daylight, Judge!

BRACK
So you find me altered?

HEDDA
A little younger, I think.

BRACK
Thank you so much.

TESMAN
But what do you think of Hedda eh? Doesn't she look flourishing? She has actually…

HEDDA
Oh, do leave me alone. You haven't thanked Judge Brack for all the trouble he has taken.

BRACK
Oh, nonsense! it was a pleasure to me.

HEDDA
Yes, you are a friend indeed. But here stands Thea all impatience to be off, so au revoir Judge. I shall be back again presently. [*Mutual salutations. MRS. ELVSTED and HEDDA go out by the hall door*].

You may have realized by now that the possibilities with the BECs are many and that constant practice with them will bring more ideas for variations on the above exercises.

Understanding what each Body Energy Centre does in response to your focus, breath, attention and intention is paramount. The more time you spend breathing into each Centre the better, as it is only practice that will bring you to a level of expertise in the use of the BECs.

Exercise Five: Using the BECs with Non Realism, working with two characters.

So how can the BECs work with non realistic plays such as Samuel Beckett's *Waiting For Godot*? Let's just look at the first section of this play.[14]

Breaking this text into units is slightly more difficult and depends very much on your rationale for ending one unit and beginning another. I have selected two sections to work with from Act 1 for the purpose of exploring the different BEC choices.

ESTRAGON			VLADIMIR		
BEC	Unit 1	Unit 2	BEC	Unit 1	Unit 2
Crown	>		Crown	*	
Mind	*		Mind	o	
Throat	o		Throat	o	
Heart	*		Heart	*	

---

[14] http: //samuel-beckett.net/Waiting_for_Godot_Part1.html.

Solar	*	Solar	o
Belly	o	Belly	*
Root	o	Root	*

Taking the first unit, you could explore the following:

- Giving Estragon a leaking Crown BEC immediately suggests his mind energy is going straight out to the heavens. Having his Root and Belly open gives him an earthy groundedness, which he is able to communicate through an open throat. Closed Mind, Heart and Solar ensures that the body energy is only emerging through the lower half of his body and throat. Playing with this configuration should offer several character choices, postures and vocal qualities. For instance, the voice will sound quite different depending on which other Centres are open. If you are not getting the quality of character you are after, you can easily try closing the Throat and opening the Mind or opening the Solar and closing the Root.

- Having a closed Crown keeps Vladimir much more down to earth, and with an open Mind and Throat he is able to communicate his ideas well. However, with closed Root and Belly he is cut off from a deep rootedness to the earth while exuding a great deal of importance of self via the Solar BEC. Once again, you can play around with these configurations.

- You are also working for the first time with two characters using the BECs, this will offer many more possibilities as you become receptive to the BEC state the other actor is offering at different stages of the text. It is a little like a dance where either actor can lead, block, return the energy or transform it. Once you become familiar with the BECs you can then really 'play' with them during performance, keeping it fresh every night.

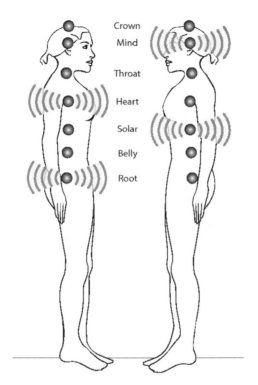

Figure 12. The body on the left is working with
Heart and Root BECs and the one on the right with
Mind and Solar BECs. Image by Shanti Portia.

WAITING FOR GODOT

Section 1

*Estragon, sitting on a low mound, is trying to take off his boot. He
pulls at it with both hands, panting.*

He gives up, exhausted, rests, tries again.
As before. Enter Vladimir.

ESTRAGON:
(*giving up again*). Nothing to be done.

VLADIMIR:
(*advancing with short, stiff strides, legs wide apart*). I'm beginning to come round to that opinion. All my life I've tried to put it from me, saying Vladimir, be reasonable, you haven't yet tried everything. And I resumed the struggle. (*He broods, musing on the struggle. Turning to Estragon.*) So there you are again.

ESTRAGON:
Am I?

VLADIMIR:
I'm glad to see you back. I thought you were gone forever.

ESTRAGON:
Me too.

VLADIMIR:
Together again at last! We'll have to celebrate this. But how? (*He reflects.*) Get up till I embrace you.

ESTRAGON:
(*irritably*). Not now, not now.

VLADIMIR:
(*hurt, coldly*). May one inquire where His Highness spent the night?

ESTRAGON:
In a ditch.

VLADIMIR:
(*admiringly*). A ditch! Where?

ESTRAGON:
(*without gesture*). Over there.

VLADIMIR:
And they didn't beat you?

ESTRAGON:
Beat me? Certainly they beat me.

VLADIMIR:
The same lot as usual?

ESTRAGON:
The same? I don't know.

VLADIMIR:
When I think of it.....all these years.....but for me.....where would you be.....(*Decisively.*) You'd be nothing more than a little heap of bones at the present minute, no doubt about it.

ESTRAGON:
And what of it?

Table 9

ESTRAGON			VLADIMIR		
BEC	Unit 1	Unit 2	**BEC**	Unit 1	Unit 2
Crown	>	*	Crown	*	>
Mind	*	o	Mind	o	*
Throat	o	o	Throat	o	o
Heart	*	*	Heart	*	*
Solar	*	o	Solar	o	*
Belly	o	*	Belly	*	o
Root	o	*	Root	*	o

You might notice that Estragon has the same BEC choices in the second unit that Vladimir had in the first and vice versa. This should give both actors good practice as well as understanding how the same choice can affect a different body.

I would suggest running these two units three or four times in order to give you enough time to feel the effect of each Centre on:

- **Interaction**
- **Text**
- **Voice**
- **Posture**
- **Gesture**

Section 2

VLADIMIR:
(*gloomily*). It's too much for one man. (*Pause. Cheerfully.*) On the other hand what's the good of losing heart now, that's what I say. We should have thought of it a million years ago, in the nineties.

ESTRAGON:
Ah stop blathering and help me off with this bloody thing.

VLADIMIR:
Hand in hand from the top of the Eiffel Tower, among the first. We were respectable in those days. Now it's too late. They wouldn't even let us up. (*Estragon tears at his boot.*) What are you doing?

ESTRAGON:
Taking off my boot. Did that never happen to you?

VLADIMIR:
Boots must be taken off every day, I'm tired telling you that. Why don't you listen to me?

ESTRAGON:
(*feebly*). Help me!

VLADIMIR:
It hurts?

ESTRAGON:
(*angrily*). Hurts! He wants to know if it hurts!

VLADIMIR:
(*angrily*). No one ever suffers but you. I don't count. I'd like to hear what you'd say if you had what I have.

There are also many possibilities within one short piece of text and just working with one BEC.

VLADIMIR:

(**Throat ***) Sometimes I feel it coming all the same.
(**Throat >**) Then I go all queer. (*He takes off his hat, peers inside it, feels about inside it, shakes it, puts it on again.*) How shall I say? Relieved and at the same time…(*he searches for the word*) . (**Throat o**) appalled. (*With emphasis.*) AP-PALLED. (*He takes off his hat again, peers inside it.*) Funny. (*He knocks on the crown as though to dislodge a foreign body, peers into it again, puts it on again.*) Nothing to be done.
(*Estragon with a supreme effort succeeds in pulling off his boot. He peers inside it, feels about inside it, turns it upside down, shakes it, looks on the ground to see if anything has fallen out, finds nothing, feels inside it again, staring sightlessly before him.*)
(**Throat >**) Well?

Concluding Remarks about using the BECs

I think it is worthwhile noting that much of this work evolves into an intuitive realm after a while, and actors find themselves moving from one Centre to another without a rigid map or design. Like everything, when new, these exercises are merely a start until the idea of the BECs and states of Leaking, Open and Closed are as much a part of your repertoire as notes are to a singer.

Once a scene gets going and the actors have been working with the BECs for months, it can be a little like a dance or a tennis match with each actor responding to the others' choices.

Working with the BECs requires repetition, focus and conscious use of breath. This takes time. It might take you a month of daily work with one BEC before you feel you have any mastery with it. By mastery I mean being able to call that Centre into play at will. Eventually the idea is to be able to call any Centre into play at any moment of the performance, keeping the body energy alive and active every night. As you master the BECs you will find many different ways of engaging them with other actors and audience.

The key to the BECs is to work with the breath and the imagination to realize the existence of these Centres within your own body. Only through daily repetition over months will you gain deep knowledge and understanding of how these Centres work in you and it will be different from how they work in anyone else's body. Eventually you will find that you automatically start to make choices from the Centres without needing to go into analytical states first, which is why you need to be mindful and thorough at the beginning. Your body will learn the states of consciousness attached to each Centre and that knowledge will become part of your tool box.

On playing the role of Charley in Arthur Miller's *Death of a Salesman*, MFA actor Matt Sullivan was asked to wear a 'fat suit' which he feared would "muffle my work", particularly as he was focusing on the Root and Belly BECs. "My fear dissolved quickly as I got used to the appendage of cloth and quickly learned that I could radiate the Centres from beneath it quite well. The concentrated expression from the lower Centres informed my articulation of the upper Centres as I called on them. With success in the Root and Belly I had begun to make intelligent use of the rest".[15]

---

[15] Ibid.

Figure 13. Matt Sullivan as Charley in *Death of a Salesman.*

An important observation by Matt is that by learning to work initially with one or two Centres, he could apply that knowledge to the rest. I think this is a useful approach since mastering all seven Centres in one production is a tall order and could easily confuse you. Start simply, stay with what is working for you and allow your body to teach you by handing over to it. "Put your consciousness into different areas. For example, do not consciously think about where to put your feet; with a choice for that area your consciousness is in your feet".[16]

In the above quote and in sections of his book *The Transpersonal Actor,* Ned Manderino explores the idea of placing consciousness into different parts of the body. The BEC approach also requires placing your consciousness into each Centre you work with. Manderino talks about inner organs communicating actions,[17] which is exactly what occurs when the BECs are engaged and each Centre

---

[16] Manderino 1989: 124.
[17] Ibid.

is interconnected with the surrounding organs, glands, nervous and circulatory systems. You cannot engage your Mind BEC without the brain, ears, nose, eyes and all connecting pathways being affected. Much of the new age information on the chakras suggests that working with the chakra system benefits health. I do believe that this is also the case with the BEC system, which is an adaptation of the chakra system specifically for use within the rehearsal room in training actors.

One of the key differences between the chakras and the BECs is the idea that you as an actor are working with two sets of energy Centres: your own and the characters.

You may have realized by now that the possibilities with the BECs are many and that constant practice with them will bring more ideas for variations on the above exercises.

Understanding what each Body Energy Centre does in response to your focus, breath, attention and intention is paramount. The more time you spend breathing into each Centre the better, as it is only practice that will bring you to a level of expertise in the use of the BECs.

Using imagery that works for you will definitely assist in BEC work as Matt discovered:

> There was a great leap forward in the Fall term of 2005 in the combination of a new, more focused effort with the BECs in Drama 221 with Jade. With some fits and starts in selection of material, I fell back to using Shakespeare, the role of Aaron in *Titus Andronicus*. The Root and Belly BECs began as stones which were lifted by a bursting heart until they dangled beneath my opened Throat blaring out the anger of my impotent position in the drama. In the end Aaron was floating back to the ground with a beaming, radiating Crown BEC. These Centres were opening and closing, spinning and pulsing almost exactly by command.[18]

---

[18] Matt Sullivan. MFA actor, Department of Theatre and Dance, University of California, Davis. 2005.

Putting your consciousness into the core of the Centre you are working with can be fast and easy, or difficult and lengthy. No two bodies are alike and each body has its own unique set of challenges.

MFA actor Paula Dawson documents her process for developing the character of Macbeth

"After finding an initial model for Macbeth's body as that of warrior, I then attempted to fill that body with intentions. I looked to the BEC system to inform Macbeth's physicality and movement. Macbeth's character is so very complex and his journey within the play so extreme, the BECs engaged could not be limited to a static few. All of Macbeth's BECs are engaged in a variety of ways throughout the play. Macbeth's energy at the beginning of the play is ruled by the Root, Belly and Solar BECs. His throat must always be engaged purely from the point of having to deliver Shakespeare's text. Macbeth is never timid about expressing himself. His Heart BEC is never completely closed nor does it leak. Yet it is not always completely open. In certain scenes, Macbeth's Heart BEC does open, particularly during Lady Macbeth's descent into madness and at the moment of her death. After this point, I deliberately closed it tightly in moments to enable him to deliver lines such as, ...I have lived long enough..." However, Macbeth's Heart BEC cannot remain completely closed for long".

"Macbeth's Mind and Crown BECs also become engaged at different points in the play; in fact spin him out of control at certain points. When he engages the murderers, he is all Mind, using his wit and calculation to manipulate the murderers into accepting his offer. He is also completely aware that he is manipulating them. However, Macbeth's other BECs, e.g. Belly, Solar, Heart, often operate in conflict with his Mind, muddying his judgment and compromising his strategic abilities. Macbeth does not have the clarity of thought and vision of Richard III for example, his other BECs, operating in overdrive, get in the way".

"I engaged Macbeth's Crown BEC at a difficult moment in the play for me as an actor, during Macbeth's final visit to the witches and at different points throughout Act V. In Act V, Lady Macbeth is in the midst of her madness; Macbeth's fellow thanes have turned against him, yet he still believes in the Witches' final prophesies, holding on to them even as his world falls down around him. Macbeth himself crosses back and forth between madness and lucidity, faith and despair. Using the BEC system in this instance required that each of Macbeth's BECs be engaged and disengaged in rapid succession, not always in a linear model."[19]

Summary

The use of the BECs is a transformative process. Breathing consciously, with intention into each of the Body Energy Centres awakens the body in a way you might not have imagined. A large key is to surrender to the body and to the amazing information it already has stored in so many layers, levels and dimensions within. It will take months and years of practice, intention and attention, not unlike training for any art form, sport or career. I think the challenge will always lie in the subtle nature of the work as it is very hard to see the Centres grow and develop, even when we feel them strongly. The judgment of a quality of inner work lies solely in the actor's hands. The energies from the Centres are unseen and impossible to analyze from a scientific standpoint. Actors have relied on intuition and unique creative responses for decades without having to prove or document their inner process. Acting relies on a trust beyond the walls of the rehearsal room; a trust in the ability of the audience to read and discern meaning from mere looks, sighs and moments of pure silence. Can we affect this space between the actor and audience by training in such a way that we can consciously send out rays of intention towards each other? Can the actor work with the subtle body and master it enough to weave tendrils of intended dreaming into the projected fabric from the audience?

---

[19] Paula Dawson was cast as Macbeth in a production directed by MFA directing student Emily Davis in the Department of Theatre and Dance, University of California Davis 2007.

CHAPTER FOUR

The Technique of Shamanic Journeying

I see theatre as a sharing of altered spaces, a transmission of sorts and certainly an event containing transformational elements. Although the idea of Shamanism poses as many questions for an actor as it might hold answers, it is a practice that has at its core, connectivity to energies and forces that swirl around and within us, including forces of nature, dreams, spirits and thought forms.

In 1990 I attended my first 'shamanic' workshop, which took place over three days and was run by a Scottish woman (I regret I do not remember her name) who had been trained by a Native American shaman. Thirty people built a sweat lodge, gathered large rocks for heating the lodge and built a fire to heat the rocks. Once in the sweat lodge, no-one was allowed to leave as our teacher beat a drum for over five hours. Fear of death through loss of air soon merged into a highly altered state where I felt 'merged' with the other participants, resulting in a loss of my sense of 'self' as my entirety seemed to collapse into the whole body. A part of me then began 'journeying' as it searched (as directed) for totem animals, signs and symbols of meaning.

When the flap of the sweat lodge was pulled back and the cool night air rushed in, it was like a feeling of being reborn. I crawled through the earth into the night and lay back to look at the stars: nothing was the same. After showering, we all met in a large circle for the rest of the day and were taught how to construct individual circles for 'a night of fear'. The 'night of fear' was literally sitting in a circle of stones I had created using ritual and a sense of the sacred, and calling in my fears to experience and analyze throughout the night. This exercise also took me into altered states and various parts of self I had not entered consciously before. It reminded me of the 24 hour improvisations I had taken part in as a member of KISS, or being lost in bushland without food or water for three days while hiking in Wilson's Promontory in Victoria's far south. My first experience of theatre watching KISS perform also had the effect of creating an 'altered space' that seemed to be magically shared by both audience and actors. To lesser degrees I had experienced altered states of consciousness in meditations and prolonged periods of strenuous physical work, but none so vividly. It is this 'traveling sense' of shamanic practice that interests me: the ability to move into other dimensions of reality with full awareness, using all senses.

In order to understand how Shamanism and actor training inter-relate, it is important to cover some of the foundations of what Shamanism is, both historically and currently. One of the earliest recorded researchers into aboriginal Shamanism was Polish cultural anthropologist, Mary Antoinette Crispine Czaplicka. Her work on Shamanism in Siberia, reflected in a publication entitled *Aboriginal Siberia*[1] was used by Mircea Eliade for *Shamanism: Archaic Techniques of Ecstasy.*[2]

The word ecstasy comes from the Latin root *ex statis*, to stand outside oneself. The term Shamanism itself was defined by Eliade as a technique of ecstasy.[3] In all Tungus languages (spoken by Mongoloid people throughout Western Siberia) this term (saman/shaman) refers to persons of both sexes who have mastered spirits: who at their will can introduce these spirits into themselves and use their power over the spirits. Shamans are mostly healers who are in contact and work creatively with the supernatural forces that aid them in their work. I feel it is important to note that historically, shamans themselves did not define Shamanism in this way. As much

---

[1] Oxford: Clarendon Press 1914.
[2] Eliade. Routledge & Kegan Paul, London 1964.
[3] "A first definition of this complex phenomenon, and perhaps the least hazardous, will be Shamanism = Technique of Ecstasy". (Walsh 1990: 10).

of the information about hunter gatherer societies was passed on orally, it is very difficult to determine the precise nature of Shamanism throughout thousands of years and very different cultures. "Archaeological evidence indicates the presence of shamanistic rituals as early as in the bronze age (Lee 1981: 2-3); some writers like Covell (1981), who do not distinguish between Shamanism and animism, go so far as to say that Shamanism antedates all historical records and has its origins in the Paleolithic".[4]

Shamans have existed in many different cultures around the world, including Siberia, Tibet, China, Australia, Africa, America, Korea, Japan and Hungary over thousands of years with many different types of the Shaman emerging. Whilst realizing the aspects of Shamanism that interest me in terms of actor training are only small parts of a larger overview, I feel it is important to note that the inspiration for the idea of Shamanic Journeying came from my experiences of contemporary shamanism, which draw from some essences of what we know of Shamanism as it existed in the past.

The craft of the actor as a shaman includes consciously engaging with the subconscious matter of life or perhaps mastering the stuff of dreams on behalf of the people. Shamans will often go 'below' the standing idea of consciousness, go deeper into realms often labeled 'unknown' because we cannot see them, and retrieve certain answers, wisdoms and ideas for their people. I think understanding shamanic consciousness could be a key to understanding these energies and might facilitate an 'observer' consciousness in the actor similar to Chekhov's 'Higher I' that can see and feel these energies as they pulsate between us and, as a result, engage these energies to affect the act of theatre.

The historic divorce of these elements from the beginning acts of theatre is nicely described by Sue-Ellen Case who writes:

> At its rebirth, theater emulated the Christian narrative, emerging from its liturgy. It did not spring from transformational rites, but as a plotted narrative with certain

---

[4] Heinz Insu Fenkl article, *Dancing on Knives: An Introduction to the Politics of Sexuality and Gender* in the journal, *Korean Shamanism*.

characteristics of change resulting in a happy ending. Had
acting been understood as ritualistic and transformative, it
might have found consonance with different traditions in
the world and different cosmologies.[5]

Regardless of my cultural heritage, I have always felt the forces of
nature and responded to thought forms hurled my way both
intentionally and unintentionally, as well as sensed a potential power
with harnessing these energies and using them to facilitate
connectivity to others. An underlying concept of Shamanism is that
we are all part of the one energy grid, map or source, whether called
God, Great Mystery, Allah or Nature. It has parallels with
Theosophy, particularly Blavatsky's Third Principle, which deals
with wholeness and completeness, that everything is part of a whole,
which we cannot fully comprehend, but we can be certain exists. All
that we think, feel, and do is not only part of who we are, but part of
the universe. Even the universe is part of something greater: it is
limitless and infinite.

Theosophy and Shamanism also share the concept that everything
(humans, animals, flowers, planets and stars, etc.) is made not only of
matter as the scientific world knows it, but also of spirit.[6] When
working with actors and theatre students in Australia, America or
Europe, it is clear that we all sense something other than the physical
at work, in our daily lives, in the rehearsal room and on the stage. In
fact, many students easily move into detailed discussion of the
supernatural, spiritual or sacred and admit experiencing moments of
telepathy, awake dreaming, altered states and trance. It is this notion
of Shamanic Consciousness through the technique of Shamanic
Journeying that I propose adding to the developing realm of actor
training theory and practice.

The ability to consciously move beyond the physical body is the
particular specialty of the traditional shaman with focus on an
ecstatic trance state "during which their soul is believed to leave their
body and ascend to the sky or descend to the underworld".[7] The

---

[5] Case 2007: 8.
[6] Ellwood, 194: 13.
[7] Walsh 1990: 23.

shaman makes use of spirit helpers, with whom she communicates, all the while retaining control over her own consciousness. These journeys may take the shaman into other realms, higher levels of existence, to parallel physical worlds or to other regions of this world. Shamanic Flight is in most instances an experience of an inner imaginary landscape, reported to be the shaman's flight beyond the limitations of the physical body.[8]

> In order to journey to the other dimensions of existence a shaman induces an altered state of consciousness within herself similar to a state of self-hypnosis. While in this shamanic trance she is in complete control, is consciously able to enter into non-physical reality where she visits the alternative realms of existence, communicates with and controls spirits, gains information, retrieves souls, and makes subtle changes in reality which may affect the physical world.[9]

Many religions, new age practices and ancient rituals involve this quality, seeing it as a desirable state where communication between one reality and another, imagined or dreamt, can take place. "Shamans know about energy and how it works both in the environment and the human body…they know about the spirit body and how to communicate with it".[10]

Shamanic Ecstasy

This is a state of exaltation in which a person stands outside of or transcends his or herself. Ecstasy may range from the seizure of the body by a spirit or the seizure of a person by the divine, from magical transformation or flight of consciousness to psychiatric remedies of distress.

---

[8] These methods for exploring the inner landscape in a fully conscious way are what informs the Shamanic Journeying exercise developed over five years by myself and the actors working on each of the three projects of *Hedda Gabler* in 1994, *The Golden Age* in 1996 and *Alabama Rain* in 1999 for actor training use.
[9] Joseph Bearwalker Wilson in 1978. Copyright, reprinted by permission of the author.
[10] Stevens & Stevens 1988: 11.

Joseph Bearwalker Wilson,[11] a self confessed contemporary shaman and early Wicca leader, gives one of the clearest and most useful explanations of three types of Ecstasy in describing the qualities of the altered states that can be experienced in the Shamanic Journeying exercise. The following is a breakdown of Wilson's description.

A. Shamanic Ecstasy.
Shamanic ecstasy is provoked by the ascension of the shaman's soul into the heavens or its descent into the underworld. These states of ecstatic exaltation are usually achieved after great and strenuous training and initiation, often under distressing circumstances. The resulting contact by the shaman with the higher or lower regions and their inhabitants, and also with nature spirits, enables her or him to accomplish such tasks as: accompanying the soul of a deceased into its proper place in the next world; affect the well-being of the sick and to convey the story of their inner travels upon their return to the everyday awareness.

B. Prophetic Ecstasy
The prophet literally speaks for God or a Higher Being.

C. Mystical Ecstasy
The mystic reports an overwhelming divine presence where the direct knowledge or experience of the divine ultimate reality is perceptible in two ways, emotional and intuitive.

The ecstatic experience of the shaman goes beyond a feeling or perception of the sacred, the demonic or of natural spirits; it involves the shaman directly and actively in transcendent realities and lower realms of being. These experiences may occur in the dream state, the awakened state, or both. Dreams, and particularly, lucid dreams, often play a significant role in the life of a shaman or shamanic candidate.

Although our present societal structures are described as 'Post-Shamanic' by anthropologists, this approach to actor training suggests a re-visiting of the idea of the shaman as a tremendous

---

[11] 1978, 1995. Joseph B. Wilson.

source of inspiration for the use of imagination and expanded consciousness for the actor.

More specifically, a society may be said to be 'Post-Shamanic' when at least six of the following eight conditions have been met:

1. Shamanic ecstasy is still present, but light trance techniques are also used to access the Otherworld.
2. Agriculture and some forms of manufacturing/crafts have replaced hunting and gathering as the primary basis for the economic life of the community.
3. The society has developed a highly stratified social structure and very specialized occupations.
4. Religion and spiritual methodology have become more fully developed and can no longer be properly referred to as 'archaic.' This is especially important for rituals, ceremonies and ecstatic techniques which had traditionally been the domain of the shamans.
5. Mystical ecstasy and intuitive visions have become at least as important esoteric experiences and doctrines as shamanic ecstasy, ascent and descent in the religious and spiritual life of the community.
6. The shaman is no longer the primary escort for the souls of the dead into their place in the next world. This role generally is performed by the priest or clergy through ritual.
7. A professional clergy regulates the religious life of the community.
8. Other forms of healing, divining and counseling are present and have replaced shamans as the primary provider of such services.

Trance States

Dr. Jeanne Achterberg, noted author, educator and Professor of Psychology and Director of Research at the Institute of Transpersonal Psychology, California, suggests that the ability to attain and control a trance is the result of cumulative conditioning and mental training, suggesting that we train our mind to respond in accordance with our will to be able to develop a deep trance. This is done by daily practice and it may take some time and effort to establish that ability, but once you have it you will be able to maintain it by practicing only once or twice per week; if you stop practicing entirely your ability will gradually lessen. *The breathing techniques of the BECs are an excellent stepping stone for working with trance states.*

When you go into any trance you gradually progress from ordinary consciousness into deeper levels. It is convenient to have a means of measuring the depth of your trance, so the paragraphs that follow outline some of the characteristics found at various depths. Bearwalker has divided the depths of trance into four major sections, and, using terms borrowed from the hypnotic sciences, called them the Hypnodial, Light, Medium, and Deep trance states.

In the *Hypnodial Trance* you progress from ordinary consciousness through the following steps:

- feeling physically relaxed;
- drowsy;
- your mind becomes relaxed and you may feel apathetic or indifferent;
- your arms and legs start to feel heavy;
- you may have a tendency to stare blankly; and
- have a disinclination to move your limbs.

In the *Light Trance* you progress to:

- a reluctance to move, speak, think or act.
- experiencing some involuntary twitching of your eyes, mouth or jaw.
- feeling a heaviness throughout your entire body and a partial feeling of detachment. You may also experience visual illusions.

The Light Trance has similar properties to the beginning of the Shamanic Meditation Journey; the breathing becomes slower and

deeper, and your pulse rate slows, your body becomes heavier and feelings of detachment from the present reality occur.
In the *Medium Trance* you definitely recognize:

- that you are in a trance and may experience partial amnesia unless you consciously choose not to.
- more sensitivity to variations in atmospheric pressure and temperature changes.
- as you border this and the Deep Trance you may experience complete catalepsy of your limbs or body. In other words, if your limbs or body position are changed you will leave them in the new position until they are changed again.[12]

Often illusions of touching, tasting, and smelling can occur while in this state.

In the *Deep Trance* you can:

- vividly experience the sensation of lightness, floating, or flying.
- recall lost memories and experience age regression.[13]

The Deep Trance is what you might experience in the 'Submerging' stage of Shamanic Meditation Journeying. You can experience total sensations of existing in another place or world, where it all seems as real as this current reality. You can 'see,' 'hear,' touch' and 'smell' the world you have journeyed into: the landscape of the play, and the character's world. In this state you can also merge into the character and move through her world experiencing life as she would.

---

[12] 1978, 1995. Joseph B. Wilson.
[13] Ibid.

Surrendering

There is a notion of surrendering when moving into trance states, an idea of almost being possessed by an altered state of self. Brian Bates addresses this aspect of actor training with considerable insight when he writes, "For most of us, the sensation of being taken over by an alien being, having our body possessed by an outside "personality," would be terrifying. We would fear that we were going mad. But for some actors, possession is not only what they experience, it is what they seek to experience".[14] Surrendering is a key factor for the following exercise, as it is a journey into consciously unknown spaces; we can easily block great imaginative creativity by assuming we know what to expect or only being open to what we think will happen. It is this element of risk that asks us to be more heroic, able to accept anything and everything that comes to us while on a Shamanic Journey. I like to think of the image of Alice falling down the well when I think of a Shamanic Journey. The fall seems out of control although she can focus on potions on shelves around her, and is able to slow the fall when interested enough to try one. She has surrendered to the fall but is also 'present' enough to explore the world of the fall and to choose potions without knowing their consequences, much the same as actors on Shamanic Journeys as describe later on in this chapter.

Shamanic Journeying

Shamanic Journeying is a technique drawing its inspiration from the many reconstitutions of the idea of shamanism. Dr. Jeanne Achterberg states in her article entitled *The Shaman: Master Healer in the Imaginary Realm:* "The shaman is plugging into a data bank that can be known in the normal, waking state of consciousness".[15] Achterberg also writes that "Medical historian, Gordon Risse (1972) claims that in the state of consciousness used in shamanism, mental

---

[14] Bates, B. 1987: 69.
[15] Jeanne Achterberg. Ch. 6 in *Shamanism* compiled by Shirley Nicholson 1990: 108.

resources are employed which modern persons either no longer have access to or are not interested in using".[16]

Shamanic Journeying trains actors to enter deeply into their imagination, to learn to trust what comes up as information from these journeys and to apply their experience in these deeper realms to their character. If we look at the following section from a journey recorded by the actor playing Rachel in *Alabama Rain*, it is clear that she is developing a useful background for her character that she can use during performance.

> I walked into the kitchen and Pheenie was baking, then I looked outside because you said look for the well, so I looked outside and there was this barn outside and I looked at Pheenie who nodded her head and I went outside down the stairs. There were really old, white rickety stairs at the back and this white gauze door...I went to look in the barn but I was really scared because I knew it would be dark inside...there was nothing there really just some hay and it wasn't really as dark as I thought it was and then I had to run back for dinner. [17]

When onstage, the actor is able to visualise the house, the barn and what home life is like. She has made the space a tangible habitat through information provided by the journey that did not occur in the text. An actor who journeys regularly into the landscape of her imagination, where entire worlds offer endless material and ideas will have the opportunity to develop a richer, deeper and more interesting and engaging character.

These dimensions and depths are rarely tapped in present Western actor training exercises and techniques which tend to focus more on text analysis, motivation, action and impulse. The approach of Shamanic Journeying accesses the actor to depths and dimensions of self that are more universal, beyond the conditioning of the cultural mind.

---

[16] Ibid.

[17] Excerpt from an actor's shamanic meditation journey in *Alabama Rain* by Heather McCutchen, Belvoir Street Theatre, Sydney 1999.

> In every role, at every show the actor must create not just
> the conscious but also the unconscious part of the life of the
> human spirit....only a tenth of our life is lived on a
> conscious plane.[18]

One interesting example of accessing Shamanic Journey states is a series of experiments conducted in 1977 by Dr. Felicitas Goodman, a psychological anthropologist, with graduate students from Ohio State University. Goodman was investigating the relationship between controlled posture and trance experiences. The exercise involved asking the students to adopt the positions of "selected body postures where the religious context seemed self evident".[19] Each posture was drawn from different meditative disciplines including shamanic and aboriginal art. For example, students copied the exact posture, stance and attitude in a picture of an Australian aboriginal elder pointing a bone at another tribesman who had disobeyed the law of the tribe. Apart from the discovery by Goodman and the students that many of the postures released specific energies within the body, they also found that most of the postures were conducive to shamanic journeys where other realities were consciously entered and experienced.

The reports of these journeys are very similar to the journeys experienced by students and professional actors using the Shamanic Journeying exercise to find their character. For example, the following accounts are from four different people in very different situations and countries who experienced forms of shamanic trance and journeying.

> 1. I felt that I was rising up right away and saw some spirits
> dancing. I saw a river flowing downward toward a mountain,
> so I entered it, became a fish and followed its flow. I arrived in
> a misty forest; I left the river and started walking among the
> trees. Suddenly I saw a black wolf. It had a white spot. I
> merged with the wolf and then became part of the mist.[20]

---

[18] Stanislavsky 1962: 166,167.
[19] Goodman 1988: 54.
[20] From an account by a student working with Shamanic Trance Postures with Felicitas Goodman in 1987. (Goodman 1988: 54).

2. I looked around and saw a monkey who stared at me then pointed at a snake that was just about to strike. It bit me and as the poison went into my system I felt immense heat. It passed through me and I was myself again. Next to me swam a fish that showed me its family and invited me to join them. I felt that the fish was telling me 'all is one, I am the same as you'.[21]

3. I am entering a wet, muddy land, it is a faraway place. I have never been here before. I am becoming the earth, it swallows me, in a huge sucking action, I am gone, underneath the soil – and then I am spat out. Now I see my character, in the distance, she dances, she is covered in mud. All that is clearly visible is her vibrant orange hair. Her movement is wild and frenetic one minute and then soft and controlled the next. A deer nudges me and tells me it is time to leave now.[22]

4. Once we went into the meditation/journey I was raring to go. The images and colors were coming before they were said. And each had a feeling in my "body", yet I could step out and see from above also. When I met *Wanda* after going through the tree, I was very surprised that she didn't just look like me in the wig and the costumes from the actual production and she was not exactly what I had pictured when I read the play. Suddenly she had one breast. The other was flat. And then the flat one became a gaping hole. Out of the hole came a bird. Then a small colorful Pelican. And then I put my eye into the gaping hole and took a look inside and said "we're all the same in here" and Wanda said "yes, but we're not." When I asked her if she had a secret, there was nothing she hadn't already shared with me. Or maybe the gaping hole in her chest was it and she had shared it before I asked. And there was a wave of

---

[21] An account by Tracy Burton, a Theatre Media student working with Shamanic Journeying with the author on the production of *Hedda Gabler* by Henrik Ibsen in Bathurst, New South Wales, 1994.

An account by Claude Widtmann, a Theatre Media student working with Shamanic Journeying with the author on the production of *The Golden Age* by Louis Nowra in Bathurst, New South Wales, 1998.

physical and emotional heart to heart connection and sadness when I had to leave.[23]

Actors using the Shamanic Meditation Journey technique to travel to the world of the play experienced the landscape clearly and often had powerful experiences with their characters. Steve Mizrach writes in his article *Ayahuasca, Shamanism, and Curanderismo in the Andes*: "Many claim their 'soul flight' takes them to familiar locations, which are close-by, and that they navigate among landscapes using recognisable landmarks". He goes on to say that many Andean shamans using the hallucinogenic herb Yage, experience the following:

1. The feeling of separation of the soul from the body and taking flight.
2. Visions of jaguars (interpreted as positive), and snakes and other predatory animals (usually thought to be negative).
3. A sense of contact with supernatural agencies (Andean demons and divinities).
4. Visions of distant cities and landscapes (thought to be clairvoyance).
5. Detailed reenactments of previous events (thought to be retrocognition.) [24]

Although this altered state of consciousness is sometimes accessed or catalyzed by the use of a powerful hallucinogen, it seems that the journeys of the Andean shamans and the student's not using drugs have several aspects in common. They are:

1. The notion of a journey from one reality to another which appears as real as the one left.
2. Visions of and encounters with animal entities that either assist or challenge the traveler sometimes resulting in a

---

[23] An account by Laurie Smith MFA actor working on a character in Advanced Acting class at UC Davis, California 2005.
[24] Ibid.

'shamanic death' where the traveler is reborn by being killed by the animal.

3. Sensations of flight, sometimes as a bird, disembodied or in their own body.
4. All five senses are active in the 'imagined landscape'.
5. Retaining of the 'conscious state' throughout the journey.

The Shamanic Journey Exercise

The Shamanic Journey ideally comes after the Body Energy Centre work which opens and prepares the body for deeper exploration. As you build a character in rehearsal and performance, you are drawing from sources both "real" and imagined. The facts that exist within a script – details that the playwright provides, evidence that the dramaturgy uncovers – live in conversation with the interpretation and imagination of each person on the creative team. Likewise, each time you enter the rehearsal room or the performance space, you are re-imagining the character that you play, the life that she leads – based on the collective efforts of all involved in the process.

Each one of us has experienced imagining the life of our character in some shape or form. Perhaps we recognize this when a certain line pops out at us or really makes sense to us for the first time. Perhaps we make a physical choice in rehearsal that helps us see or feel the impact of the subtext. The following Shamanic Journeying techniques are designed to amplify or heighten your ability to imagine the details of your character's life; perhaps even more importantly, Shamanic Journeying creates a palate of images and feelings from which you can draw when you enter rehearsal and performance.

In this sense, Shamanic Journeying differs from mere daydreaming or even intense script analysis. In a state of increased relaxation and focus, you are invited to join your character in her world and imagine a series of interactions and experiences unedited. While you are using the knowledge that you have already gathered from the script, you now have the opportunity to imagine new layers of your character's life, which will enrich your performance experience and increase your impact on the audience.

First Stage: Relaxing

Start with a good thirty minute or more warm up, such as trance dancing. For those of you who are not familiar with Trance Dance, it is a contemporary form of dance that combines elements of shamanism, ritual and altered states using particular sound tracks with heavy drumming and rhythmic components. Often a blindfold is worn and the room darkened, dancers surrender to the beat of the music and to their body allowing movements to occur they might not have experienced before. There should always be an observer present to watch out for potential 'wild' dancing that might interfere with the dance space of another participant. There is quite a lot of information available on the web under Trance Dance.

Put a mat down on the floor; put your notebook beside the mat, plus something to keep you warm. Lie down on the mat and relax into it. The following text is my usual way of working with this exercise; ideally each teacher and actor will find their own way into this journey.

Note: As the actor, you will know your character, the given circumstances and story beforehand in order to journey into the landscape of the play and be met by your character who will teach you about them.

Listening to soft music, preferably accompanied by a natural soundscape – lie down on your back and feel yourself sinking into the floor. I use the following text or similar to lead the actors into a state of deeper relaxation.

You feel your feet getting heavy, like lead, you cannot move them they are so heavy. Your ankles and calves are so heavy you couldn't lift them if you tried; they are like lead. Your knees and thighs feel so heavy they might sink through the floor. From the waist down your body is heavier than lead, you cannot move it at all. Your hips, belly and lower back are becoming heavy, sinking into the floor with the weight, your chest, back and shoulders are too heavy to move. From the neck down you are like lead. Your neck and throat, face and back of head are so heavy; your whole body is sinking through the floor, too heavy to move. All you can do is to observe your breath as it moves freely through your body.

Second Stage: Entering

Some of this seems repetitive; however it is important to be consistent with this particular exercise as it acts as a 'portal' or 'doorway' between the two worlds of the rehearsal room and the imagined landscape of the play and your character. You will feel safer and more relaxed as you become familiar with the images below of the countryside and the following descriptions of the river of colors. If these remain consistent, you can then see how your ability to focus intently on a color develops over the weeks. These exercises will eventually deepen your experience of the different vibrations of each color *and therefore different levels of consciousness that accompany these colors.*

You now find yourself lying in a field in the country. It is a beautiful sunny day with blue skies and a gentle breeze. There is a river nearby, and a large tree near you. You hear birds in the distance and feel the soft breeze on your face. The river is calling to you; you get up and move to the river. It is crystal clear; you can see the soft river bed. You step into the river, it is warm and soft. You know you can breathe in water and lie down on the river bed feeling safe and relaxed. Your breath is flowing through you as the river moves by you. Let the water flow past you, over you, through you. Your body and the river are flowing as one.

The river is now changing color; it becomes a brilliant white color. You breathe this color in to every cell in your body until your whole body becomes this brilliant white color. The river then brings the color red; the shade and depth of this color is up to you.

*The color red moves gently through the soles of your feet, up through your;

ankles,
calves,
thighs,
 hips,
buttocks,
belly,
chest,
back,
shoulders,
arms,
hands,
neck,
throat,
chin,
mouth,
nose,
ears,
eyes,
mind and finally
the crown.

*Repeat the above section for each color.

The color red fills your entire body and then moves out through the top of your head.

Soon you see a beautiful orange light traveling up the brook. It trickles up into your toes, your legs, your arms and torso, into your head. The light fills you entirely and then trickles right out the top of your head, moving along with the river. Your body is filled with the light, which travels right on up and then drains away.

Now there is a beautiful yellow light traveling up the brook. It enters through your feet and toes and flows right up through your body and out the top of your head. The yellow light passes through the body then leaves through the top of the head. Now there is a green light approaching, slowly trickling up through your toes and the soles of your feet, it moves into every cell in your body and then out through the top of your head.

Now approaching is a blue light, which enters into your toes and feet, filling your entire body with its rays and passing out the top of your head. The blue light passes through and now there is an indigo light moving up the river, filling your toes, your legs, your arms and torso, up into your head and right out through the top of the head.

Third Stage: Submerging

Note: I often use different music for this stage; it could involve drumming or just a different tempo.

Move to the side of the river and climb out onto the bank feeling relaxed and refreshed. You return to the spot where you were lying down and see the great old tree there. You notice in the trunk of the tree there's a door. You move to the tree and open the door, stepping inside onto the spiral staircase and closing the door behind you. You descend the stairs to the door at the bottom. You open this door and step out into the landscape of the play. You close the door behind you. Remember you can find this door at any time simply by thinking 'door'. It will appear in front of you. Your character is there waiting for you. She is smiling at you as she greets you. She will show you her world. She might take your hand or just walk with you. Observe what she is wearing, eyes, hair, hands. Accept everything she tells or shows you. Allow her to show you her world. Notice the landscape, the sounds, the smells, the colors.

- For the next five minutes (or whatever time you feel is necessary) just allow your character to show you her life.

- (After five minutes). Ask your character questions, about their fears, what makes her laugh, what does she want? Ask any question that comes to you. Listen, observe. (Allow another 5-10 minutes).

- Ask her if there's anything more she needs or wants to tell you before you leave. (Two minutes, approximately).

- Thank her for the journey: tell her you will come again. Let her lead you back to the door or if she leaves, follow the path back to the door. You will see the door in front of you. Open it, step through and close the door behind you. Ascend the spiral stairway to the door at the top, open the door and step out into the countryside, closing the door behind you.

- Lie down in the field feeling relaxed and inspired. You can see the beautiful blue sky, hear the birds and the river. A soft breeze blows across your face. Gently you will bring yourself back into the rehearsal room. You are lying on the mat very relaxed and you can remember much of the journey. Gently stretch your hands, feet, legs and arms. Take a few minutes to locate yourself and when you are ready write down as much as you can about the journey in your journal.

Note: It is important not to put full light on immediately as the actors are still in an altered state of consciousness. I usually fade the music out slowly also.

Fourth Stage: Emerging

Take at least 10-15 minutes to write and get some water if you need. Then sit in a circle and share any aspect of what happened to you in the journey. You might talk about the colors in the river, meeting the character, events that occurred in the journey, the river or the field. I encourage everyone to be open and not to judge as this information is coming from a very different part of your body.

Often the first journey is challenging and some might go to sleep or drop out of awareness. This is common, be assured that some part of your body was journeying. Often by the second and third Shamanic Meditation Journey you will find a greater awareness and consciousness occurring.

Each time you visit, the character might be a different age, in a different mood, wanting to share different things. The more often you journey, the easier it becomes to enter that world of the play on this level.

Understanding Shamanic Journeying

The notions of trance, dream states, meditation and creative visualization have been around for the past one hundred years or more in different forms and appearing in literature from different disciplines. It has been proven that we are highly susceptible to suggestion when we are in various stages of trance or dreaming. The Shamanic Journey exercise is designed to help the actor access some deeper places of consciousness, some that are almost 'behind thought' as Hélène Cixous would say.

The idea of 'behind thought' leads us into the vast landscape of knowledge beyond the boundaries of what we usually call 'mind'. The 'mind' has been placed above all other forms of gathering and holding knowledge and certainly privileged over the 'instincts' of the body or our feelings. The idea of 'mind' has been developed into the idea of 'rational' and 'logical', rising to the giddy heights of 'scientific'. Thought has become classified and its usefulness determined by whether it is from the body or from the mind.

The Shamanic approach is to access knowledge from the body and to prioritize this knowledge over the knowledge of the mind or the more rational, logical, analytical self. These are all related to states of consciousness and it just depends on how we value what we know and whether we can listen to these other sources of knowing. Milton Erickson,[25] an *American psychiatrist* specializing in medical *hypnosis*, believed that the unconscious mind was always listening, and that suggestions could be made which would have a hypnotic influence. Erickson spent most of a year with Aldous Huxley, the

---

[25] Erikson was founding president of the American Society for Clinical Hypnosis and a fellow of the American Psychiatric Association and the American Psychopathological Association.

writer of *A Brave New World* amongst others, observing Huxley in a state of what he called "Deep Reflection." Each day Huxley would sit in a quiet place, bow his head, close his eyes and move into a medium trance where he was aware of what was happening on the outside but also engaged in the alternate reality within. There are many similarities to Huxley's meditative/trance state and Shamanic Journeying and for this reason I have included a fairly long passage from Erickson's writings on these experiments, which took place in the early 1950s in California.

> In his deep trance Huxley found himself in a deep, wide ravine, high up on the steep side of which, on the very edge, I sat, identifiable only by name and as annoyingly verbose.
>
> Before him in a wide expanse of soft, dry sand was a nude infant lying on its stomach. Acceptingly, unquestioning of its actuality, Huxley gazed at the infant, vastly curious about its behavior, vastly intent on trying to understand its flailing movements with its hands and the creeping movements of its legs. To his amazement he felt himself experiencing a vague, curious sense of wonderment as if he himself were the infant and looking at the soft sand and trying to understand what it was.
>
> As he watched, he became annoyed with me since I was apparently trying to talk to him, and he experienced a wave of impatience and requested that I be silent. He turned back and noted that the infant was growing before his eyes, was creeping, sitting, standing, toddling, walking, playing, and talking. In utter fascination he watched this growing child, sensed its subjective experiences of learning, of wanting, of feeling. He followed it in distorted time through a multitude of experiences as it passed from infancy to childhood to schooldays in early youth to teenage. He watched the child's physical development, sensed its physical and subjective mental experiences, sympathized with it, empathized it, rejoiced with it, thought and wondered and learned with it. He felt as with it, as if it were he himself, and he continued to watch it until finally he realized that he had watched that infant grow to the maturity of 23 years.
>
> He stepped closer to see what the young man was looking at, and suddenly realized the young man was Aldous

Huxley himself, and that this Aldous Huxley was looking at another Aldous Huxley, obviously in his early 50's, just across the vestibule in which they both were standing; and that he, aged 52, was looking at himself, Aldous, aged 23. Then Aldous aged 23 and Aldous aged 52 apparently realized simultaneously that they were looking at each other, and curious questions at once arose in the mind of each of them. For one, "Is that my idea of what I'll be like when I am 52?" and, "Is that really the way I appeared when I was 23?" Each was aware of the question in the other's mind. Each found the question of "extraordinarily fascinating interest," each tried to determine which was the "actual reality" and which was the subjective experience outwardly projected in hallucinatory form. To each the past 23 years was an open book, all memories and events were clear, and they recognized that they shared those memories in common, and to each only wondering speculation offered a possible explanation of any of the years between 23 and 52.[26]

The concept that we have many different states or layers of consciousness that can be utilized in different ways connects with the different states of trance that shamans can enter, as well as the many dream states we have all experienced.

Creating a Character Using Shamanic Journeying

Building a character from the information received during Shamanic Journeys has added a layer of material that has been created at a different level of consciousness, or whilst in a different state of awareness.

The following passages are experiences of Shamanic Journeys experienced by undergraduate and graduate acting students and professional actors in Australia and the United States over a period of ten years and three productions. They might help to give you an idea of the range of experiences and dream-like images that were encountered.

---

[26] From: The collected papers of Milton H. Erickson, volume I; Irvington Publishers 1980: 128.

These extracts of journeys experienced during shamanic meditations show many similarities to those experienced by shamans. The most prevalent shamanic experience in the journeys experienced by the actors, in all three productions using these methods, is that of 'shamanic death'. This is a death of the self in another reality, often caused by an animal consuming the body. The actors are told of this occurrence and the likelihood of this happening. We talked about it a great deal and came to the understanding that it was an empowering event of rebirth and not to be feared.

1. Shamanic journeys experienced by an actor during the *Hedda Gabler* rehearsal process in 1994. Directed by the author at the Ponton Theatre, Charles Sturt University, Bathurst, New South Wales 1994.

"I started my journey and suddenly was in the same tunnel (to a previous journey) but this time it seemed large. I could feel the stones under my feet. I walked slowly sensing movement in many directions. A wolf passed me but answered no question. Suddenly above me was an enormous bat that at first wrapped me up in its wings safely but suddenly I couldn't see the lights at the end of the tunnel. I began to struggle with the bat. I wanted to get away from it. I struggled but the more I struggled the worse it got, I thought I would die from lack of breath. The bat kept getting tighter and tighter. At last I gave up. I accepted that I would die. As soon as I did that the bat disappeared. I was free. I walked out feeling at peace. It was dusk at my magic place, I looked around and saw a monkey who stared at me then pointed at a snake who was just about to strike. It bit me and as the poison went into my system I felt immense heat. It passed through me and I was myself again. Next to me swam a fish that showed me its family and invited me to join them. I felt that the fish was telling me 'all is one, I am the same as you'. Above my head my eagle circled. As I left the pool it landed in front of me. I asked it if it had a message for me. It nodded and flapped its wings three times. It flew off. I looked behind and saw a very small cat. I asked it the same question. It nodded and for one instant looked like an enormous panther. It then drew with its paw five straight lines! I was then alone so I came back to my body". [27]

Eagle Journey. "...it (the eagle) wanted me to follow it, I did. I climbed up the cliff; it was hard and painful work. I wondered if I could fly but my body seemed too heavy and grounded. I reached the top of the cliff and still the eagle flew on. I followed, falling and tumbling down a rocky cliff. Then I was in a kind of rock desert that seemed to go forever and ever. I kept climbing, falling and hurting myself. I was nearly dead with thirst and exhaustion. I wondered if the eagle would stop. It was like it was my master and I was its slave. I had to follow it, I had no choice. Slowly I came to terms with the fact that the eagle would keep flying until I died. Yet I kept following it. I was owned body and soul by this eagle. I felt great fear, I knew that I would die if I kept following the eagle and I wondered if I would ever come back to physical reality. Somehow I doubted it. I had to stop following the eagle. Suddenly I could see a cord joining me to the eagle. It was joined from my waist to its tail. I tried with all my strength to break it I couldn't...I must break it, I must free myself. I tried with all my strength to no avail. I was scared, angry then submissive by turns.

I would fight with all my strength then fail and give up. At last I tried to cut it. I felt my time was running out...if I hadn't cut it by the time I was brought back to the physical I was in trouble. Somehow I knew this. In one final outburst of strength I sent a big lightning bolt through the cord and broke it. I was free. I had the strength after all. I turned away from the eagle and began to walk back to my magic place, suddenly I felt something following. I turned to look, it was the eagle. As I looked at him I knew it had been a test and I had passed. I walked back to the mountain and the eagle let me know that I could fly if I could give up all fear. But I hadn't the strength left and I had to get back to the physical world so I climbed back to my body. Later on, in another journey I flew. I have never ever had a dream about flying and now I have flown". [28]

---

[27] Tracy Burton, student actor/assistant director, *Hedda Gabler,* 1994.
[28] Ibid.

2. Alabama Rain by Heather McCutchen. Directed by the author at Belvoir Street Theatre, Sydney 1999

The story revolves around five sisters existing on a dry, barren property in Alabama, USA, where it hasn't rained for forty years. In the first five minutes the eldest, PHEENIE, leaves on a quest for water and LAURIE LAURIE dies as a result of her sister's departure. The three remaining sisters, MONTY LOU (who has been pregnant for 19 years), RACHEL and DALLAS (the youngest) struggle with their fears and the ghost of LAURIE LAURIE who refuses to leave them in peace. There is a well they are all afraid to visit which is a key issue as they know their only hope lies deep in the well.

1. Lee Rickwood[29] (LAURIE LAURIE)

Describes meeting her character on a Shamanic Journey who flies her through the sky and in a dream-like sequence of images Lee learns about the landscape in which the character dwells. "I hold on to her waist and she soars me through the sky, from high up above I saw the boarding house (in the play) and the well and then the cemetery and I was swinging on a front gate before I got called to dinner...and then there was a fence on the other side and beyond that I saw all these skeletons like dead animal skeletons so it didn't really appeal to me to go out wandering because it was all full of skeletons and death and I thought I might end up like that. I was too scared to go to the well because walking through the cotton was scary so I found a big road in the middle of it with lots of corrugations in the dirt...wooden fences, slats and all very old and tumble down grey colour and dried out. That's the landscape I saw."

Lee used all of the images above that she experienced in the journey to fill the stage with this imaginary place that had come to life through the journey.

---

[29] Australian actor playing the part of Laurie Laurie in *Alabama Rain* by Heather McCutchen.

Figure 14. *Alabama Rain* by Heather McCutcheon. From left to right. Lee Rickwood, Angela Morrison and Tash Beaumont. Photo by Corrie Ancone.

2. Belinda Armstrong[30] (RACHEL)

"I walked up to the porch and into the house completely unnoticed. I didn't even say hello to Mum, she was just sitting talking to all these boarders and they were men. I walked into the kitchen and Pheenie was baking, then I looked outside because you said look for the well, so I looked outside and there was this barn outside and I looked at Pheenie who nodded her head and I went outside down the stairs. There were really old, white rickety stairs at the back and this white gauze door…I went to look in the barn but I was really scared because I knew it would be dark inside…there was nothing there really just some hay and it wasn't really as dark as I thought it was and then I had to run back for dinner. I came back and I was sitting next to Laurie Laurie and Monty was on my right hand side, we kept

---

[30] Australian actor playing the part of Rachel in *Alabama Rain* by Heather McCutchen.

giggling and we got in trouble for giggling. Laurie Laurie got in trouble for not helping Pheenie with dinner and Pheenie got in trouble cause something was too hot. There were two men there and so we were all eating with our heads down. I started eating before Mum said the prayer, she didn't yell at me, she just stared at me.

We were all just sitting there and I just couldn't wait to eat I was so hungry. I shared a room with Dallas…I woke up to a breaking glass sound and our window overlooked, like we could see over the front porch, over the dirt road and corn fields and stuff and I could hear her (Mum) screaming at this man to get off the property…then I had dreams of Dad and us being so happy in the house and Dad was home and everything was happy and gold and just beautiful. And then I went to the well and had to climb down into it…like stairs going down…it was a big dark hole, like a mining cave and I noticed Laurie Laurie was there and I asked her what she was doing and she said she was doing a spell. And when I asked her what for, she said it is a secret and if I tell the well will take it from me".

Figure 15. *Alabama Rain*. Tash Beaumont as Dallas and Belinda Armstrong as Rachel. Photo by Corrie Ancone.

3. Lee Rickwood (LAURIE LAURIE)

"It was the wolf, a wolf howling was what woke me up and it was full moon and there was a guy out there with a gun, and he was in love with Mum. But she didn't want anything to do with him and he had a gun and you know he was threatening and violent and there was a lot of tension in the house and I just saw him there shouting, I didn't see how it was resolved or anything, he was just shouting with the gun, spit down his face, very angry, shouting at my Mum".

4. Tash Beaumont [31] (DALLAS)

"I was going to your room and you weren't in bed which I kind of knew you wouldn't be and you were outside dancing with this invisible whatever (Laurie Laurie) and I was sitting on the porch watching you…like a waltz, I had on a dress today, it was too big for me and comes to like my knees, faded beige floral dress." I went to visit the well, it was a really traditional well this time, like a fairy tale with a bucket…kind of normal, it was very cute, it wasn't very scary. The feeling of fear was like a cliff face, if you get within a couple of feet you start to think 'oh no,' but when you're a couple of metres away it's no big deal".

5. Lee Rickwood (LAURIE LAURIE)

"The church, it was a little stone thing, very dirty and wooden pews and we were all going there, a bit like Madeline, you know all kind of straggling in one line with Mum and her Mum, Grandma, in front and when we got to the church, when you get to the church no-one ever thinks about not going, its just not the done thing, no-one even thinks about it although I've got the feeling that I don't want to be here and that all of my sisters are feeling the same thing as well but you just do it and Mum and Grandma just do it. Then they were singing in the church and they were going 'ssshhaaaalllll weeee gaattthhher aaatttt tthhhheeee rriiiivvvveeerrr' and cracking up laughing at each other, kind of going off at each other in this real kind of high crazy voice. I

---

[31] Australian actor playing the part of Dallas in *Alabama Rain* by Heather McCutchen.

was trying to sing like a bird, and feel my throat and with the lips but in the sound of the voice was the tweeting. Then all this came really quickly to me, I had a whole lot of time, so I thought well okay what am I going to do now – and there I was flying and that's the joy because she is dead and she can fly now and I hadn't even thought of all that before so I was just flying. And then the prayer was 'Now I lay me down to sleep bless my soul the Lord to keep, if I should die before I wake bless my soul the Lord to take'. And she said it to me with the same voice, with a kind of tweet in it".

Note:Lee used the information from this journey to create a bird-like character who was fond of 'perching' and whose voice had a definite tweet to it. Her character Laurie Laurie sang the same song Lee heard in her journey "Shall We Gather at the River" during the play.

Figure 16. *Alabama Rain.* Lee
Rickwood as Laurie Laurie.
Photo by Corrie Ancone

6. Belinda Armstrong (RACHEL)

"We all sort of waddled in (to the church) all holding hands and there weren't many people there and I remember just trying to look at Mother all the time. The Minister was really old and he had a bald head with grey hair at the back and this huge white coat on with one of those pastor things that they wear. I was just staring at him and he was talking about death and I didn't know what he was talking about so I looked out the window and there were all these pink storks flying and then irises. Mother was talking to the Minister and he was saying 'how are the girls' and she was saying 'oh they're fine, they're just fine, just fine, thank you very much for asking' and we walked home. Then these boys came past in this old pick up truck, this really old pick up truck and the dust flew up everywhere and they were yelling at Monty because Monty was pregnant. And they were yelling some ya-hoo or something and Mother was like 'look forward girls, keep walking, don't look, don't ever let 'em see you cry Monty' and all the girls were standing there holding each others hands, like freaking out, just holding hands and walking straight and couldn't move".

3. **Myth, Propaganda & Disaster in Nazi Germany and Contemporary America by Stephen Sewell.** Directed by the author at the Mondavi Center for the Performing Arts Studio Theatre, University of California, Davis, 2006.

EVE
- "Eve is two characters. Her inside/outside, her old/new, her perception and her reality. When I arrived at the bottom of the tree, she was shifting between two images of herself to show me that she had made a distinct choice to change her physical appearance at some point in her adult life. She was moving between red, wavy hair that was short and shoulder-length, with brown freckles and very dark, long thick hair and powder-colored skin. She is hiding. She is passing in some way. She has a Midwestern (a bit nasally) sound to her voice that is somewhat suppressed but comes out when she is in a more casual space, like at home. She is a private person

and likes her private moments within public spaces; a downtown NY park bench, where the wind blows so hard she feels that she can't be seen; an orange and brown booth in a seedy café where she wouldn't likely be so no one would pay attention to her; using the big heavy metal weights at the gym where no one would see her because all of the women are in the aerobics studio...She was very poor in the past, so, she says, there is no discontinuity between the authenticity of her former self and the successes of today – there is no big crisis about "making it" as she would if she had been raised with privilege. That, she says, is something you only feel when you've always had things, always had food, always had clothes, always had toilet paper. If you haven't and now you do – what's the problem? The message and the goal and the intent and the compassion are still there as they always have been. What is the major crisis with the means by which we arrive, as long as we aren't hurting anyone?

Figure 17. Mary Elizabeth Anderson, playing Eve in *Myth Propaganda and Disaster in Nazi Germany and Contemporary America.*

- I met Talbot while traveling in India. But I had met him before – I had seen his image before on a book cover while browsing in a bookstore traveling elsewhere but I never told him that and it had taken a while for me to remember or know that myself. I thought he was much younger than he was – or, I felt like he was much younger, more my age, but I was ultimately very attracted to the fact that I knew he was some 10 or so years older. Yet, at that time, I felt like I had something to offer him that he hadn't known before, another kind of knowledge, despite the fact that he was so well read, well traveled and had known many things. But my perspective had been, until now, entirely unknown to him despite the fact that when he met me I felt entirely familiar to him. As if he had been waiting for me...

- What's so difficult now is that he has somehow forgotten what it was about my perspective and approach to life that was so true for him at the time – I'm still pursuing the same things, but my approach has lost value to him now, and he sees me as just another opponent at times... It is hard to believe that someone who seemed to listen so carefully at one time in our past, and me not even trying to be anything other than me, feels like he's already heard everything I've got to say and I can yell these days and I can't be heard. I can't be heard."[32]

- "Very stream of consciousness-esque. It was a stone interrogation room; he wouldn't let me see him. He showed me what he had seen, the things he'd done...'the horror', kind of like 'Apocalypse now'. First image of two towers falling all different angles, then him raping an Arab woman and killing her husband. He is so hurt by doing these terrible things.

- He wanted to show me his friends, I saw Guantanamo Bay/Abu Ghraib, men with bags over their heads...that torture is the only way he relates to people; through interrogation, a frightening place.

---

[32] Mary Elizabeth Anderson, MFA student at University of California, Davis.

- Comic books, he wanted to be a super hero as a kid, wants to save people like Captain America, sees the world in Black and White, Good and Evil. Why did that make me want to cry? Maybe the loss of innocence...loss

- Violent Tom & Jerry cartoons keep appearing.

- Started losing it when we were on color blue in the river, went on my own journey, completely left the arena, did I fall asleep?

- He took me to where he lives rather than his office, no art, bare apartment, made me peanut butter and jelly. Very stiff, very confident, sure of every step and every move.

- I tried to give the man a gift but he refused it and told me to go away. He likes boxing, he has a bench and bar in his room."

Figure 18. Matt Rapore,[33] playing The Man with Victor Toman asTalbot
in *Myth, Propaganda and Disaster in Nazi German
y and Contemporary America.*

[33] Undergraduate acting major at University of California, Davis.

Summary

Shamanic Journeying is a structured way of moving through varying levels of trance. The first stage of **Relaxing** is very much like the Hypnodial Trance as you become drowsy, heavy and reluctant to move. The second stage, **Entering** is like the Light Trance where a deep heaviness takes over your body and the thoughts in your mind have less power over determining your conscious state. The third stage of **Submerging** moves you through the Medium Trance to the Deep Trance where your breathing slows down, your body becomes deeply heavy and inert and your consciousness is no longer in the room but with the character in the landscape of the play.

This is also a state of surrender in order to access a deeper place of creativity and imagination, a place where part of you merges with the very core of the character. When you are called back into the room in the last stage of **Emerging** it will be challenging the first few times to try to bring the two worlds of the journey and the reality you are in together. This does get easier with each journey as you assimilate the information, images and feelings you discover while on the journey. However for the first three or four times you attempt the Shamanic Journey I suggest having someone observing who will make suggestions, talk you through and bring you back. Making sure you spend at least twenty to thirty minutes assimilating and perhaps sharing some of your journey experience with others is also a good idea.

The information gathered in these journeys not only deepens your understanding of the character but also permeates other layers of consciousness within the body in such a way that the character becomes embedded within these layers, resulting in a richer, more multi-dimensional portrayal of the character.

CHAPTER FIVE

Playing the Exchange:
The Actor Audience Dynamic

My first powerful experience of theatre occurred in Adelaide's State Theatre in 1980. I was attending a performance of Oscar Wilde's *Salome*, performed by actors from the International Research Theatre Group KISS from Holland who were mostly trained with Jerzy Grotowski's methods. Something occurred in that transaction between my seemingly passive body and the very active actors' bodies. It was more than feeling touched, more like feeling deeply included and somewhat like receiving a' transmission'.

Various definitions of 'transmission' define it as a system, an act, a process that transmits messages, information, codes or energy through a medium. The auditorium, in a theatrical event, might even be seen as a 'petri dish' for exploring energy exchanges between actors and the audience: a site where we are engaged with the process of transmission both as spectator and actor. It seems theatre practitioners have long been intrigued and concerned with these transactions and transmissions. Antonin Artaud wrote in 1946, "The theatre is a passionate overflowing, a frightful transfer of forces from body to body. This transfer cannot be reproduced twice".[1]

While watching Salome dance the seven veils, I felt taken away from myself and transported to an altered state wherein I was somehow magically a part of a collective whirling, dancing thought form. A

---

[1] Artaud 1946 in Derrida 1995: 250.

passionate transfer of forces indeed, although certainly not 'frightful,' I observed my physical body sitting there in the auditorium while my awareness or consciousness had expanded out across the audience, across the holy bridge to the performance itself. At the same time, the performance was moving *in* me. This awakening experience was far too powerful to be dismissed as mere imagination, leading me to ask what else is at work beyond my physical body. I also question whether this is unalterably automatic or do we have a choice as to how we engage various levels of our consciousness with these transmissions?

We know psychologically that processes such as Transference and Projection occur in both the rehearsal room and the auditorium; ideas such as Mimesis, Alterity and Otherness coming out of the newer field of Performance Studies have all been investigated, explored and applied to this petri dish of performance. However, apart from understanding the process of performance in a more complex way, the ideas of consciousness, transmissions and energy exchange are all still best described by both Stanislavsky and Chekhov.

In his book *An Actor Prepares*, Stanislavsky writes;

> Besides listening I want you now to try to absorb something vital from your partner. In addition to the conscious, explicit discussion and intellectual exchange of thoughts, can you feel a parallel interchange of currents, something you draw in through your eyes and put out again through them? It is like an underground river, which flows continuously under the surface of both worlds and silences and forms an invisible bond between subject and object.[2]

Stanislavsky explored in depth these ideas of transferring forces via the notion of 'communion' in this book, spending an entire chapter on descriptions, exercises and images in an attempt to explain the interchange of currents. Throughout this chapter, Stanislavsky (via the characters of the director and the student actor), investigates notions of soul, spirit, Energy Centres and communion with self as

---

[2] Stanislavsky 1936: 201, 202.

well as others. What is most interesting is his persistent enquiry as to the nature of soul and the detailed descriptions to the actors as to how they can identify whether they are communicating 'soul to soul'.

One of the dilemmas in attempting to clarify what these exchanges are and how an actor can be trained to consciously engage in them, is the clear lack of a current 'scientific foundation' upon which to build and develop this clarification. I have turned to the esoteric sciences influencing Stanislavsky in his time, in particular the writings of Theosophists such as C.W.Leadbeater, A.E Powell, Alice Bailey, Annie Besant and of course Madam Blavatsky. Their combined metaphysical enquiry into the unseen forces that seemingly connect us all has provided us with an entire framework with which to view the energetic transactions between human beings.

At the same time that Theosophy was on the rise under the leadership of Madam Blavatsky, (1831-1891,) writers and thinkers such as George Ivanovitch Gurdjieff, (1872-1949), Peter D. Ouspensky, (187-1947) Alistair Crowley (1875-1947) and Rudolph Steiner (1861-1925) were also intently investigating this ethereal cosmic matter loosely rolled into the realm of the esoteric. Stanislavsky (1863-1938) was developing his acting techniques around the same time that the Theosophists in particular were highly focused on the energy body that accompanied the physical body in the form of various silhouettes that mimicked the physical body, almost a series of extending body outlines. As the energy body extends away from the physical body, so the consciousness or awareness of the body extends.

This movement could be described as shifting from coarse to finer matter, a matter built up of minute electric charges, positive and negative, connected together by the invisible universal element called the ether. The etheric body might be seen as a kind of interface with the larger body of finer matter surrounding us. In his book *The Power of the Rays: The Science of Color-Healing* in 1951, S.G.J. Ouseley suggests that the ether is the transmitter of the essential life-forces and that this cosmic organizing force is susceptible to control by

Mind and Will; mind controls life and life controls matter.[3] Perhaps because he was living in Russia at the same time as the emergence of these esoteric and philosophical developments, Stanislavsky's acting system relied heavily on the ability of the actor to imagine a world and through the intention of thought and power of the mind to create that world which such a force that we as audience have no choice but to believe that world exists before our very eyes.

Much of Chekhov's technique relied upon the power of imagination or the ability of the mind to create strong thought forms which then influence the perceived reality. Chekhov's exercises of Radiation and Atmospheres also heavily depended on the actor's ability to completely trust the unseen realm of imagination and what they construct there. These exercises called upon the actor to project an intention through the air towards another, be it the audience or a fellow actor. The actor was asked to create a believable atmosphere filled with another reality to present to the audience, an atmosphere that must convey to and connect with the bodies in the auditorium. Is the idea of 'atmosphere' connected to S.G.J.Ousley's and other theosophist's ideas of 'ether'?

One important question underlies the fact that when both Stanislavsky's and Chekhov's acting systems moved beyond the borders of Russia, all notions of esoteric training were left behind. Why did all the exercises of yoga, meditation and references to theosophy and the esoteric disappear? I suspect that due to the beliefs of the time, much of the accompanying information to the core of these systems was lost along the way, as both Stanislavsky's and Chekhov's acting techniques arrived in America, England and Australia minus the underpinning of an awareness of energetic systems at play within the body. More recent research has brought to light Stanislavsky's attraction to Yogic principles and recent fresh translations of his rehearsal notes have identified many passages copied in Stanislavsky's handwriting from Yogic books by Ramacharaka.[4]

---

[3] Ouseley 1951: 37.
[4] William Walker Atkinson, (1862-1932) writing as Ramacharaka, helped to popularize Eastern concepts in America, with a focus on *Yoga* and abroadly interpreted *Hinduism*.

Stanislavsky through the character Torstov in *An Actor Prepares* writes; "I have read what the Hindus say on this subject. They believe in the existence of a kind of vital energy called Prana, which gives life to our body."[5]

It seems that the MAT actors were working with the invisible matter that connects us all to each other and to nature, using terms such as 'intention,' 'imagination' and 'circles of attention'. Andrew White's research importantly reveals an underlying deep commitment in Stanislavsky's work to the spiritual/yogic and theosophical philosophies and approaches.

White posits:

> Given, however, the presence of important Yogic elements in the system at its very inception, a full understanding of Stanislavsky's technique is impossible without knowledge of the intersections between his system and Yoga. Borrowing from Yoga, Stanislavsky offers actors much more than theories about how to be more believable or psychologically realistic in their roles. He adapts specific Yogic exercises in order to help actors transcend the limitations of the physical senses and tap into higher levels of creative consciousness.[6]

Like any of us who seek to discover a language for the actor that enables her to open up to the many and varied levels of 'creative consciousness,' Stanislavsky was drawing on the available language of the time even though, as he admitted, he was also at a loss for words. In *An Actor Prepares*, the director Torstov (Stanislavsky's alias) speaks to his actors about the idea of communion "Up to this point, we have been dealing with the external, visible, process of

---

[5] Stanislavsky 1936: 187.
[6] Taken from abstract for article 'Stanislavsky and Ramacharaka: The Influence of Yoga and Turn-of-the Century Occultism on the System', in: *Theatre Topics*, Spring 2006.

communion, but there is another, more important aspect which is inner, invisible and spiritual".[7]

Torstov then goes on to say: "My difficulty here is that I have to talk to you about something I feel but do not know. It is something I have experienced and yet I cannot theorize about it".[8] Instead of theorizing, he uses a passage from Shakespeare's *Hamlet* between Hamlet and Ophelia to demonstrate what he is trying to describe.

> He took me by the wrist and held me hard; Then goes he to the length of all his arm, And with his other hand thus o'er his brow, He falls to such perusal of my face As he would draw it. Long stay'd he so. [9]

Torstov asks the actors if they can sense the 'wordless' communion between Hamlet and Ophelia in these lines and asks them whether they have ever experienced something similar; "When something streamed out of you, some currents from your eyes, from the ends of your fingers or out through your pores"? [10]

Acting is an art form unlike any other; the human body with all its dimensions, layers and senses is the prime tool with which the actor creates her art, the art of representation, of living temporarily another life as a different character on our behalf. There is an immense amount of research carried out by the actor to discover the character she is portraying. This research covers a very large amount of territory including;

- Full analysis of the text
- The culture, politics, religion and behavior of the time
- The psychology of the character
- The physical attributes of the character including posture, gestures and mannerisms

---

[7] Stanislavsky, *An Actor Prepares* 1936: 199.
[8] Ibid.
[9] Ibid.
[10] Stanislavsky 1936: 200.

- The emotional life of the character
- What drives or motivates the character, how the character thinks

Eventually all of this research synthesizes into the representation of another being in various layers of body, voice and...well, what are those other dimensions?

It is generally recognized that vibrations of unseen energy can operate at varying levels of coarseness or thickness moving right through to the highest, finest level of vibration. From music to color to science, these vibrational densities have been investigated with particular musical notes and chords, colors and infra-ray heat signatures, all being recognized by their frequency of vibration. One layer of vibrations that emanates from and acts upon the physical body is the energy of thought and how this affects the actors and the audience. "Every definite thought produces two effects: first a radiating vibration: second, a floating form".[11]

It makes sense that the more we dwell on particular thought forms, the stronger these forms become. Powell describes how vibrations in the mental body, i.e., created when we are thinking, communicate to the surrounding matter which receives this communication 'precisely as the vibration of a bell communicates itself to the surrounding air'.[12] Within this communication the mental vibration will often reproduce itself when it strikes upon another mental body. In other words, when a body is struck by a thought form, it has a tendency to reproduce a similar thought. We know the psychological frameworks of transference and projection easily transfer to the site of actor/audience exchange as a way of viewing and understanding the transfer of forces that occurs in the act of theatre. Perhaps the addition of Powell's extensive work on Thought Forms can assist further in both understanding and enhancing the actor/audience dynamic.

---

[11] Powell 1982: 43.
[12] Powell 1927: 43.

Clearly the degree to which this occurs depends on the intensity of the original thought form and the openness of the receiving mental body. When applied to the audience-actor exchange, this framework offers some exciting possibilities. Powell writes at length about the susceptibility of some people who are not thinking 'definitely or strongly', to the effect of surrounding thought forms, citing that there lies a great burden of responsibility upon those who are thinking 'strongly and clearly' as their thoughts will inevitably affect large numbers of people.

Powell also makes an important distinction about thought forms conveying the *character* of the thought but not the *subject*. "Thus, for example, if the thought form be one of devotion, its vibrations will excite devotion but the object of the devotion may be different in the case of each person". [13]

Actors spend a great deal of time in their preparation and rehearsal time creating images in their mind of the character and the world they inhabit. These 'images' are similar to thought forms, concentrated bodies of energy dwelling about and within the actor's body. On stage these thought forms are consciously projected by the actor as they inhabit the character and we as audience buy into that projection and construction of another world – even though somewhere in our minds we know it does not 'really' exist.

The following Thought Form exercise is a combination of Michael Chekhov's 'Radiation' exercise and Stanislavsky's 'Circles of Attention'; both require sending energy to the other actor and to the audience. The form of the energy might vary, particularly in terms of what it is called – prana, chi or a thought form but basically these exercises all ask the actor to conjure, design and master unseen energies and forces emanating from her body.

Thought Form Exercise

The actors enter an empty room and form pairs. They sit opposite each other with their backs against the walls (approx. 7-10 metres

---

[13] Powell 1927: 47.

apart), facing each other with their eyes open to begin with. There is no verbal communication during this exercise. Once deep eye contact is established the eyes are closed. One side then attempts to 'send' an image to the other over a time of approximately three to five minutes. The image involves a color and a shape, for instance, a blue circle, a green jagged triangle, etc. When the sender has exhausted her ability to project the image she opens her eyes and waits for her partner to do the same. When everyone has their eyes open the partners then come together in the centre of the room and share their experiences. This then opens up into a sharing of the results by the group.

Often the first time results are mixed and inconclusive and it isn't until the third or fourth time that the receivers actually receive exactly the image they're being sent. The first time I experimented with this exercise was in 1994 with the cast of *Hedda Gabler*; after three attempts the majority of participants (80%) were receiving exactly what was being sent to them. The other 20% had varying levels of reception such as receiving the color not the shape or vice versa.

Depending on the source of the vibration and possible obstacles, the thought will affect others to varying degrees. These mental/astral thought forms have a life of their own as long as they are being contemplated, received and added to. Although the audience does not go through this training with the actor, the assumption is that these consciously projected thought forms or 'radiations' will have some effect on the audience on a non-verbal level. "What name can we give to these invisible currents, which we use to communicate with one another? Someday this phenomenon will be the subject of scientific research...meantime let us call them rays".[14]

To access the state from which radiation is best achieved, the actor must relax as any mental distractions tend to create blockages. Exercises of meditation or yoga are often good warm ups to the above exercise as well as good preparations for rehearsal in general. The benefit of this kind of exercise to the actor is one of enhancing actor-audience connection. If the actor develops an ability to project

---

[14] Stanislavsky 1936: 200.

focused, designed energies and intentions to the audience, a 'bridge' of energy is established. It then becomes easier for the audience to enter the world of the play as a participant, sharing the altered reality and being truly affected on all levels.

If we are to believe that such phenomena exist, we could surmise that we are engaging daily in the creation of these thought forms daily and that it is possible to become aware of the thought forms we are sending to others and those we are receiving. Would this be a raising or expanding of consciousness, to become aware of these processes and energy forms? Or is it just pure imagination? Either way, this is the realm of the actor who is often intuitively in touch with the powers of intention, imagination and attention. Thought forms are forms of consciousness; whether they are higher or lower forms depends on the quality and nature of these thoughts. For the purpose of theatre and actor training, these thought forms can become a conscious element as part of the matrix that connects us all, the prana that flows between all living things. Stanislavsky writes:

> People communicate through invisible mental currents, through radiations of feeling, commands of the will. This path from soul to soul is the most direct, influential, valid, strong, and suitable for the on-stage transference the inexpressible, the superconscious, lending itself neither to word nor gesture.[15]

For me, there is no doubt that Stanislavsky was deeply involved in the raising of consciousness and thought about the soul, spirit and inner 'unseen' energies. He consistently engaged in the exploration of these energies, calling them 'rays', 'consciousness', invisible radiations', 'communion', 'inner currents' and 'superconscious'. His system was far more complete than what was actually carried over to America, England and subsequently many other Western countries. "Let the actor believe that these are the most effective, irresistible,

---

[15] From Vol. 4 of the Russian Collected Works, *An Actors Work on the* Role which was translated into *Creating a Role*, Routledge 1989, byHapgood.

subtle, powerful means to convey the most important superconscious, invisible things which cannot be put into words by the playwright".[16]

This book is an attempt to re-unite some of the vital missing components from Stanislavsky's and Chekhov's original systems of actor training with contemporary theories and ideas of yoga, theosophy and shamanism. These are all techniques to access the inner world and to develop 'inner communion' as Stanislavsky puts it so that the body of the actor becomes so much more than just physical, mental and emotional; it becomes a body of energy that is so much more pervasive when consciously creating an exchange between bodies.

> One word, in conclusion, about the active principle underlying the process of communication. Some think that our external, visible movements are a manifestation of activity and that the inner, invisible acts of communion are not. This mistaken idea is the more regrettable because every manifestation of inner activity is important and valuable. Therefore learn to prize the inner communion because it is one of the most important sources of action. [17]

---

[16] Stanislavsky 1965: 106.
[17] Stanislavsky 1936: 193.

Feedback on the BECs

Interview with Matt Sullivan by Mary Elizabeth Anderson.
17 May 2006 at UC Davis

"MA: Were there ways that the training that you got from the training with Jade that were useful to you?

MS: Generally in acting there are a lot of different values that I'm pulling out of there right now. One is this: the practice of BEC breathing and the specific way I had had a tremendous breakthrough and it was about the way that Jade was leading us through the breathing and the way that it is destructuring and restructuring. So, we began with, as you recall, the moving, the rhythmic moving and deep breathing. I was really straining my lungs and it was in the chest. I made a determination pretty early on that I was going to make this a severe effort. Taking from past experience with Grotowski, I automatically see a value in stressing myself. And so what that led to was a real severe beginning of the process that was very destructuring. I believe that sweat begins to break down and then the chemicals in your body begin breaking down. I'm no chemist but I can feel it, I have a sense of this. So that happens and then on Jade's cues I would begin restructuring by becoming specific with the energy Centres going from the Root up and expressing each one in an almost artificial way. She would say, "Now begin with the Root" and I would start moving my Root in a crude way but eventually that crude beginning would become more refined and become more fluid and in each Centre it would work that way. So it would begin with a crude indication, in actor terms, but if you commit to it and continue with it its the same thing as having an awkward line, it's a crude indication in the beginning but if you give yourself to it, eventually you'll make it work. As long as you're able to, it's like a little courageous act. So that had brought me to a breakthrough, where I was using my body more than I'd ever used it, especially in the Root and Belly Centres, which has been (in my thesis I refer to it as) a concrete apron for cultural reasons for physical reasons, genetic reasons, absolutely unexpressive below the heart. And that's a big breakthrough.

In *Death of a Salesman* with Charlie, I was able to articulate things in scenes an example of which would be that most often before onstage, I had done very little to express my character below, say, the solar plexus. And I believe I was now able to do that successfully in *Death of a Salesman*. I was doing that especially since I had identified for Charlie that the Root and the Belly are secure – that is his haunt, that's his security, that's where he is absolutely sound and expressive. He's almost a hedonist. So steady and so all of the basic things in life are pinned down for him and so he's able to articulate himself from that solid foundation in the Root and the Belly. What was most important was my security and my movement to start things down below. And again this is all very new to me so I'm not very articulate, but...it's clearly working in my work.

MA: I remember watching the physical breakthrough in the scene that you did.

MS: Yes! You're talking about the monologue. Yes, yes and also in taking Jade's direction. The previous year when we had worked, the technique was new to me and I was intensely skeptical. And it took me a long time to accept Jade's efforts...That was a breakthrough in the class because I gave in. It is not my instinct to allow someone to tell me what to do as an actor. I'm ok in dialogue with a director, but it's very hard for me to accept suggestions. I've been doing it a long time. I want to be sure that doesn't sound like I'm some kind of petulant actor. I'm not, but I want to know – if somebody's telling me to do something, I want to know that they know better than me what I should do and so it's difficult to accept them. For some reason, and I think it is hooked into the exercise with the BEC breathing, I think that put me in a frame that allowed me to accept...even things that I thought, "doesn't work with this character." I finally made the breakthrough of saying, "you know, it doesn't matter what you think the character is." It doesn't matter. What matters is that you just open up and let go.

MA: Would you say that you felt yourself becoming more receptive, in that sense?

MS: You know, it is funny, because I pride myself on a long acting career of being very receptive. I pride myself on...I always make sure that the director feels like I'm responding to their direction. If I sense that there's any difficulty I always go directly to them and I say, "listen, I'm taking notes... I'm taking *these* notes on the things you're telling me and I'm trying to implement them to the best of my ability. Am I failing?" If I think there's trouble, I'll go to them and say, "Am I failing? Let's talk." I take being professional very seriously. So, more receptive, yes, in the broadest sense.

MA: I notice when you talk about your professionalism – when you talk about working with a director, you use the words "responsive" and "responding" and I wonder if there is a difference between this and the idea of receptivity. The idea of taking in, because when I used to leave class after having worked with Jade – and this happened from the beginning, from the first class I took – I would walk outside and I started to notice natural beauty, I started noticing strangers on the street, the reflection of light on a person's hair...with an exceptional quality of attention. It was a heightened reception. Like my feelers were out. And this is why I keep coming back to this idea of reception. It is openness. The training helps with what some people refer to as relaxation, or increased focus of energy.

MS: I think it's destructuring. You went through destructuring of the physical. It's the same as good hard physical exercise. It's endorphins. It rearranges your thinking. There's no doubt in my mind. And it's not just that. But that's a part of it. What's important is that the artist recognizes what's happening- my initial resistance, that's the resistance of a 48 year old man who's been practicing a craft. It's like going to a carpenter who's been doing it for 25 years and saying, "You know what, let's try this other way." There's resistance there...

MA: In a company environment with continuous practice the technique starts to make sense in your body.

MS: Like what Grotowski had in Irvine. So we could take what we've been doing in class and expand that out to four or five hours and then go further and continue it. Because that's one thing Grotowski had going on. The couple of times I participated, they were doing the river and we'd dance a single step for 24 hours with breaks every three, four hours to have some water. Literally 10 minutes to have some water and get back to it. And what was happening to my spine was incredible. I had to stop because my back is so bad. I had to stop and recover. But what I was doing, what I was expressing was new stuff. And I never reclaimed it. I never picked it back up again. I went from there into film and television. Film and television you stop using the lower half of your body. It's not necessary, except in the most special shot. Everything else is useless.

MA: What would you say was the moment that you realized that you had made a physical transformation and what did that feel like? Do you remember at what point in the process it happened?

MS: I think there was a gradation of points. I think the first year of training is when I began to get the taste of something. And it stemmed from the breathing. I was going nowhere with the Shamanic Journeying. Yeah. Nowhere. And it wasn't until the breathing really started working for me…I was laying on the mat, just pouring sweat and there was enough of a breakdown of my body that I was no longer quite so resistant to whatever Jade's suggestions were. But I've got a ways to go. The things I was hearing from you, from Shelly, the places where your brains took you with the slightest cue... I was nowhere near that and by the end of the second class, I'm still in baby steps with that. But I still do the breathing. And I'm still trying to find the right music. I want the breathing exercise to go on for a longer time. I want to go far with that because it's good for you. You know, it's just a marvelous potential.

MA: I think there's something about the durational component of the training, like you're saying, the breaking down in order to take yourself to a new place. Because for me, the use value of the technique is not just in the application of the Body Energy Centres as *concepts*, but in the process of discovering the quality and nature of each BEC. And this process of discovery can only come over time.

You can see the difference when you pursue the technique long-term. At the beginning of the training process, when you are conscientiously opening and closing a particular Body Energy Centre in order to achieve an effect on a characterization, it can appear to be an interesting "trick." It is visually and audibly compelling, but you know that, as a performer, you have only begun to "find" the BEC. The real depth of the work comes from a durational investigation.

MS: That's right. And what Jade did with me in that first class – for instance, directing me to muffle my throat BEC – I think that that has a brilliant effect. And I've seen it done before, too, in different ways...Robert Cohen at Irvine identified in me the thing that has been my problem all my life and he never said a word, he never articulated it in words. He did it by practice. I was in a Shakespeare seminar with him and he had us doing Puck's line, "My mistress with a monster is in love." And he had us in a circle doing the line. And he saw me do it ... We were going to be doing Hamlet and I was on fire to do Claudius because I knew he was going to cast someone else to do Hamlet. A young kid and I was 27 years old, so I thought I'd do Claudius. So it came my turn to say it and I said, "Mymistresswithamonter'sinlove." And Cohen didn't say a word. He went on and then other people were saying it, giving their all and he came back to me and "Mymisteresswithamonter'sinlove." So Cohen handed me a piece of paper and said, "Matt, crumple that up into a tight ball." And I did. And he said, "Now stuff it in your mouth." And I did, he said, "Ok. Now, give me that line."
"RrRrRrRrR..."
"I don't understand you."
"RrRrRrRrR..."
"What?"
"RrRrRrR..."
And I got louder and louder and then finally I was leaping up and down and trying my best to articulate "My mistress with a monster is in love" through that wad of paper. And then Cohen said, "Ok, now he actually is starting to get it across, with a wad of paper in his mouth." And, you know, he just used me! He took my shitty little attitude and he was kind and nice the whole time. Grotowski did a similar thing with me but he was cruel. He humiliated me when he saw me changing the work. All I did was change the work, I talked

the actress I was working with into us changing – to have leather jackets and be drug addicts and really get this all dirtied up and he's going to love it…so we did. It was a scene between Peer and his love interest, it was a tawdry little scene in the bedroom where I was being cruel to her.

It had been a star scene, he just wanted to work on it and so we came in and we tarted it up. Here's Grotowski, Parliament cigarettes, and he says, "Jeem… tell heem to do't again." And – Jim Sloviak, this was his assistant – so Jim says, "Ok. Diane, go sit down." For some reason they knew it was all me. "Go sit down Diane." Diane just went (makes a face)…and went and sat down. And Jim said, "All right, take your pants off. Take your shirt off and your pants off." I'm in my underwear. "Ok. Now we want you to put on your rock and roll music and want you to play air guitar." And I just said, "Jim, what? I don't get it. Why."
"Shut up, Matt. Just do it."
"But…why?"
"Matt! You wanna do it or do you want to leave?"
And I said, "Ok, I'll do it." I did it. I just exploded all over the place. It was just…I want to make a long story short, I was so flippin humiliated, that I just (makes exploding noise), then Grotowski went on and talked about at length about how he is sick and tired of American banality and this notion that things have to be new and change things and you know, you come in here and you think I'm going to like you changing things. Then he kind of made me feel better by saying, "Matt actually showed a real Stanislavskian volcano here. This is a wonderful thing that we also achieved."

What I'm driving at is that's destructuring too, to a young actor, it's where the teacher can reach in…the way Jade did it and the way Cohen did it, I prefer. No humiliation. Just being wise enough and understanding enough. Having enough repose. To identify what the actor's problem might be here. Like in my case I figure Jade figured "He leans on his voice…he's leaning on his voice, so all I'm going to get out of him is through the throat so let's restrict that" I assume that's what Jade was thinking.

MA: In your Titus Andronicus monologue, you began with the Matt that we always see, standing up right with the really nice posture, extending out from the torso... and as you worked the monologue in class, you came to develop this character with a convoluted, crazy physicality and vocal quality that we had never seen...

MS: I was totally against Jade telling me to go up into my Crown at the end, I was totally intellectually against it. It didn't work for me but something about the way the class had gone and that breathing exercise, I was receptive, as a human being, not as an actor. I, Matt Sullivan, the guy, just said, "You know what? It's not worth me defending my idea of character. I want this to go well. I want to see what Jade's talking about. So I did it and it worked. That wasn't actor-director either, that was just human, I believe that's the state of mind that the training gets you in.

MA: I'm wondering how this training differs from other traditional Western models of actor training.

MS: What Jade is teaching is part of a relanguaging of Michael Chekhov, his psychological gesture. It's real. It's there, the fact is science has informed us that what Chekhov is talking about is actually scientific and he didn't know it. Body Energy Centres go right into that perfectly. His inspiration was theosophy. And so was that of Meyerhold and so I think it's just perfect...Body Energy Centres and Tai Chi. By the way, they have a common Root, so, as far as Western acting goes, what Jade is working on is, quite simply a newer approach to accessing the things an actor needs to access. A new configuration of how you're going to get at it.

MA: A different avenue or door to walk through.

MS: And it seems more and more to me that's the actor's job is access – the actor's job is learning those avenues. Accessing, I like that word, like Jade talks about Shamanism and the possibilities of channeling. What I would suggest is that there's a kind of innate spiritual thing within us (and it's also neurobiological) that channels. There are no bodies coming from the universe or anything like that. It's all in here. It's all in the electrical complex and we need to find access to it. The best actors are going to be the ones who not only find access but establish pathways."

Feedback from Four Actors who have worked with the BECs

"As I became more familiar with the BEC technique in achieving the goal to isolate and fill each Centre with energy I began to understand its physiologic manifestation's: 1.To increase the metabolic expenditure of each specified area and 2. To increase the Blood flow to those areas which fueled this flow of energy. As the experience continued I was able to direct the energy to a specified anatomical position which climaxed in the crown as I passed from the frontal cortex known for its synergistic abilities of perception and decision making to the visual perceptive region of the occipital cortex". As the sessions continued the relationship between my body and mind became more and more intimate."

Aaron Campbell[1]

"For the rest of my career, I will be able to use the BECs to clarify and illuminate character. Usually the directors won't know what I'm doing – they'll simply observe me "becoming the character," even though character is an illusion to me. If "generality is the enemy of all art" (Stanislavsky), then the BEC work is a home run for helping actors become more specific with the use of their bodies".

Jesse Merz[2]

"he work gave me the profound realization that everything I need is already within me and also the tools to unlock it all. The power I felt when my energies were aligned was extraordinary. I think this technique is an amazing one for any actor to explore."

Nikki Britton[3]

---

[1] Aaron is studying Neurobiology, Physiology and behavior at University of California, Davis. and is also a UCDMC Operating Room clinical intern.
[2] MFA actor University of California, Davis.
[3] 2007 Graduate of the Actors Centre, Sydney, Australia.

"Jade's work with Body Energy Centres addresses an aspect of the craft that is investigated all too infrequently. True, without a voice or a physical instrument, an actor is hampered, but without a deeper understanding of his or her own spiritual connection to the instrument, no amount of training will produce results. The BEC work encourages such understanding and has led me down a path that has enriched my performance no end".

Denby Weller [4]

---

[4] 2007 Graduate of the Actors Centre, Sydney, Australia.

Bibliography

Abram, D., 1966. *The Spell of the Sensuous*. Pantheon Books, New York.

Bailey, A., 1986 (1950) *Telepathy and the Etheric Vehicle*. Lucis Publishing Company, New York.

Barba, E., 1995. *The Paper Canoe*. Routledge, London & New York.

Barba, E. & Savarese, N., 1991. *The Secret Art of the Performer*. Routledge, London & New York.

Bates, B., 1987. *Way of the Actor: A Path to Knowledge and Power*. Shambhala Publications, Boston.

Bearwalker, Wilson J. http://stason.org/TULAR/new-age/shamanism.

Begely, S., 2007. *Train Your Mind Change Your Brain*. Ballantine Books, New York.

Black, L. C., 1987. *Mikhail Chekhov as Actor, Director, and Teacher*. UMI Research Press, Michigan.

Brook, P., 1987. *The Shifting Point -Forty years of Theatrical Experimentation 1946-1987*. Methuen, London.

Brook, P., 1990. *The Empty Space*. Routledge, London & New York.

Case, S.E., 2007. *Performing Science and the Virtual*. Routledge, London & New York.

Chekhov, M., 1991. *On The Technique of Acting*. Harper Perennial, New York.

Cixous, H., 1993. *Three Steps on the Ladder of Writing*. Transl. S. Cornell & S. Sellers. Columbia University Press, New York.

Cixous, H. & Clement, C., 1993 (1986, 1975). *The Newly Born Woman.* University of Minnesota Press, Minnesota.

Cixous, H., 1994. *The Helene Cixous Reader.* Ed. S. Sellers. Routledge, New York.

Derrida, J., 1995. *Writing and Difference.* Routledge, London.

Eliade, M., 1963. *Patterns in Comparative Religion.* Transl. R. Sheed. Meridian Books, New York.

Eliade, M., 1976. *Occultism, Witchcraft & Cultural Fashion.* University of Chicago Press, Chicago.

Eliade, M., 1959. *The Sacred and the Profane.* Transl.W. Trask. Harvest Books, New York.

Eliade, M., 1961. *Images and Symbols.* Transl. P. Mairet. Harvill Press, London.

Emoto, M., 2004. *The Hidden Messages in Water.* Beyond Words Publishing, Hilssboro, OR.

Franz, M.L., 1997 (1979). *Alchemical Active Imagination.* Shambhala Publications, Boston & London.

Goodman, F.D., 1988. *'Shaman's Path' in Shamanic Trance Postures.* Ed. G. Doore, Shambhala Publications. Boston & London.

Gallagher, S & Shear, J., 1999. *Models of the Self.* Imprint Academic, Thorverton (UK).

Gordon, M., 1988. *The Stanislavsky technique: Russia: a Workbook for Actors.* Applause Theatre Book Publishers, New York.

Grotowski, J., 1968. *Towards a Poor Theatre.* Simon and Shuster, New York.

Harner, M., 1980. *The Way of the Shaman.* Bantam Books, Harper & Row, New York.

Judith, A., 2004 (1996). *Eastern Body Western Mind.* Celestial Arts, Berkeley, CA.

Lachman, G., 2006 (2004). *In Search of P.D. Ouspensky.* The Theosophical Publishing House, Wheaton, IL.

Leadbeater, C.W., 1980 (1927). *The Chakras.* The Theosophical Publishing House, Wheaton, IL.

Lendra, I Wayan, 1995. *Acting (Re) Considered: Theories and Practice*. Ed. P.B. Zarrilli. Routledge, London & New York.

Lommel, A., 1967. *Shamanism: The Beginnings of Art*. McGraw-Hill, New York.

Manderino, N., 1989. *The Transpersonal Actor*. Manderino Books, Los Angeles, CA.

Mayer, D. & K. Richards, 1977. *Western Popular Theatre*. Methuen, London.

Malidoma, P., 1993. *Ritual: Power, Healing and Community*. Swan Raven and Company, Columbus NC.

Mitter, S., 1992. *Systems of Rehearsal*. Routledge, London & New York.

Ousley, S.G.J., 1951. *The Power of the Rays: The Science of Color-Healing*. Fowler & Co. Ltd., Essex.

Ozaniec, N., 1996 (1990). *The Elements of the Chakras*. Element Books Limited. Shaftsbury, Dorset.

Powell, A.E., 1982 (1927). *The Astral Body*. The Theosophical Publishing House, London.

Powell, A.E., 1983 (1969). *The Etheric Double*. The Theosophical Publishing House, London.

Richards, T., 1995. *At Work With Grotowski On Physical Actions*. Routledge, London & New York.

Schechner, R., 1988. *Performance Theory*. Routledge, London & New York.

Schechner, R., 1985. *Between Theatre & Anthropology*. University of Pennsylvania Press, Philadelphia, PA.

Shakespeare, W., 1988. *The Complete Works of William Shakespeare*. The Cambridge Text, Peerage Books.

Stanislavsky, C., 1936. *An Actor Prepares*. Transl. E. Reynolds Hapgood. Theatre Arts Inc., New York.

Stanislavsky, C., 1965. *Creating A Role*. Theatre Arts Inc., New York.

Stanislavsky, C., 1962. *My Life In Art*. Geoffrey Bles, London.

Stanislavsky, C., 1948. *My Life In Art*. Theatre Art Books, London.

Stevens J. & L. Stevens, 1988. *Secrets of Shamanism.* Avon Books, New York.

Tacey, D.J., 1995. *The Edge of the Sacred: Transformation in Australia.* Collins Dove, Melbourne, and HarperCollins, Sidney.

Turner, V., 1988. *The Anthropology of Performance.* Paj Publications, New York.

Turner, V., 1982. *From Ritual to Theatre.* Paj Publications, New York.

Walsh, R. N., 1990. *The Spirit of Shamanism.* Publisher Tarcher, Los Angeles, CA.

White R. A., 2006. 'Stanislavsky and Ramacharaka: The Influence of Yoga and Turn-of-the-Century Occultism on the System'. In *Theatre Survey* 47:1 (May 2006).

Zarrilli, P. B., (ed.) 1995. *Acting (Re)Considered: Theories and Practices.* Routledge, London & New York.

Index